MW01633807

**Richard Williams, Ed. D.**

# THEY STOLE IT,
# BUT YOU MUST RETURN IT

HEMA Publishing, Rochester, New York 14623

HEMA Publishing
P.O. Box 23977
Rochester, New York 14623

Printing in the United States of America by HEMA Publishing
Typesetting by All Pro Printers
Cover Design by Richard Williams and Adam Bradley

Library of Congress Cataloging in Publication Data:

Williams, Richard, data.
They stole it, but you must return it.
1. Black family.   2. Black Health.   I. Title
86-91239
ISBN 0-938805-00-2

This book is available at a special discount when ordered in bulk
quantities. Contact HEMA Publishing, P.O. Box 23977, Special
Sales, Rochester, New York 14623.



HEMA  Publishing,  Rochester.

*To my mother,
with love*

# ACKNOWLEDGEMENTS

I wish to thank my friends for their editorial comments. This group includes Dr. John Walker, Dalton Johnson, Janice Brown, Wanda Budd Strother, Arlene Brathwaite, Clarissa Budd, Marilyn Duncan, Susan El Rayes, Rolland Micheals, Jacqueline Hokes-Neal, Elfreda Blue, Claudia Brown, my son, Richard Williams, Jr, my daughters, Laura and Melissa Williams, and my wife, Sharon Williams.

# Contents


SECTION I — BLACK FAMILY
Chapter 1
Introduction ... 3
Chapter 2
The Black Family ... 7
What Was The Black Family Like? ... 8
What Did White America Do to the Black Family ... 9
How Did White America Choose to Destroy
the Black Family? ... 9
Chapter 3
What Did White America Do to the Black Mother? ... 15
Chapter 4
What Did White America Do to the Black Father? ... 19
How Did White America Destroy the Black Father? ... 19
The Milling Process ... 20
Chapter 5
What Did White America Do to Destroy the Black Child? ... 25
How Did White America Destroy the Black Child? ... 25
Chapter 6
Blacks Response to the Slave Experience
First Level ... 29
Coping by Fighting ... 30
Coping by Running ... 30

Coping by Compromise 32 Chapter 7

Blacks Response to the Slave Experience

Second Level 33

The Black Female and Compensation 34

The Black Male and Rationalization 36

White America and Intellectualism 39

Ego-Defense Blasting 43

Chapter 8

Relationship Development Plan 45

The Self-Fulfilling Prophecy 48

Respect 49

Communication 49

Creativity Can Build Relationships 50

Sensitivity 52

Trust 53

Chapter 9

Education Plan 55

Chapter 10

Sexual Plan 63

Chapter 11

Family Enrichment Plan 67

Chapter 12

Time and Space Plan 69

Time 69

Space 72

Chapter 13

Community Involvement Plan 73

Chapter 14

Prevention of Perpetuation of Slavery (POS) Plan 75

Chapter 15

A Word About America 81

This Generation 84

SECTION II — BLACK HEALTH

Chapter 16

Black Health 87

Good Health Plan 91

Understanding Health 91

Chapter 17

  Proper Diet    93

    Why Is Proper Diet Needed?    94

    What Is a Proper Diet?    95

Chapter 18

  Water    97

    Why Is Water Important?    98

    How Much Water Does the Body Need Daily?    98

    Water Substitutes    99

Chapter 19

  Sleep    103

    Why Are Adequate Amounts of Sleep Important?    103

    How Much Is an Adequate Amount of Sleep?    104

Chapter 20

  Fresh Air    107

    Why Is Fresh Air Important?    107

Chapter 21

  Exercise    109

    Why Is Exercise Important?    109

    What Is Proper Exercise?    111

Chapter 22

  Stress Reduction    113

    What Is the Stress Response?    114

    How Can I Control Stress Responses?    115

Chapter 23

  Killers    117

    Smoking    117

      What Happens When You Smoke Cigarettes?    118

      Children and Cigarette Smoke    118

      What Will I Gain If I Stop Smoking?    119

      Why Is It Difficult to Stop Smoking?    119

      How Can I Stop Smoking?    119

    Alcohol    120

A Final Word    123

Appendix — "Black Man"    125

References    127

# SECTION I
# BLACK FAMILY

# Chapter 1

# They Stole It, But You Must Return It

THEY STOLE IT, BUT YOU MUST RETURN IT, is an unusual title. 'THEY' refers to White America, and 'YOU' refers to Black America. Usually, the thief must take the responsibility and pay equal value for what he stole. However, with White America, this did not happen. They stole it, but you must return it.

BLACK AMERICA, you are a miracle. You are the product of the greatest survivors on earth. For any group to experience the cruelty, brutality, and wickedness that was thrust upon you by WHITE AMERICA, and survive the experience with any semblance of sanity is a miracle. But, that survival experience has left some long lasting consequences; consequences that affect BLACK AMERICANS today.

To create an effective slave system, White America focused on destroying the positive self-image in blacks, and destroying the black family structure. In the process of trying to destroy the black family, White America forced inhumane conditions on the slaves. These conditions affected the health of the black slaves. The black family has not completely recovered because many factors and behaviors from the slavery experience continue today. To understand the problems of the black family today, and to understand the health problems of blacks today, you must understand the experiences and circumstances under which these problems developed.

The purpose of this little book is to look at the slavery conditions and their affect on the black slave family, and the black family today. This book also offers methods and ways for the black family to become strong and for its members to be healthy. This is a book not only about the black family, but for the black family.

The term WHITE AMERICA refers to a specific group of caucasians living in America. Not all caucasians are in this group. White America refers to the white caucasian segment of America that advocates racial hatred and promotes social injustices. That part of America violates the American creed of freedom and justice for all. This group includes the known caucasian racist and the caucasian American who hides behind the concepts of the caucasian racist. Both groups often bypass the American system of justice when dealing with Black Americans and other racial minorities.

This group dominated the trends during the reign of slavery in America. Similar racist groups exist in America even today - groups like the Ku Klux Klan. This country is also infested with subtle racist groups. For example, as late as 1985, in'The City of Brotherly Love,' Philadelphia, Pennsylvania, subtle racism raised its ugly head on Buist Avenue to tell a black family and a racially mixed family, "You do not have the right to live in our community like other Americans because you are black." This group vandalized these couples' homes. This second group is sometimes hard to identify, but under pressure it shows its true colors.

However, thank God, there is another group of caucasians in America. These are genuinely good people. They possess a sensitivity, a concern and an appreciation for all mankind. Some members of this group led the way for the Underground Railroad for slaves. Some wrote and spoke out on the evils of slavery in America. They pressured the United States government and President Lincoln to abolish slavery. They are speaking out today very strongly against the Apartheid government in South Africa. They are joining hands together to get food and supplies for the hungry and needy around the world. These are true Americans. These are they who stand for this country's creed - liberty and justice for all.

# Chapter 2
# The Black Family

The family is the most important social unit in any society. A healthy family experience is important for one to develop and maintain social and mental health. It gives one the sense of belonging. Family members have a bond sealed by common blood. God gave the gift of family to the human race to maintain sanity and stability.

> "Then the Lord said, 'It is not good for the man to be alone. I will provide a partner for him.'"
>
> Genesis 2:18

A man without his family is like a lion without his teeth; he has the heart and he has the power, but he cannot overcome his prey. A woman without her family is like a bird with a broken wing; her ability to fly is inhibited. And worse yet, a child without his family is like a ship caught on a rough sea without a rudder.

Any system that deprives a people of its family structure, denies the humanity of that people. The developers of such a system defy the Creator of mankind and insult the Creator's creation. White America originated such a system in its slavery scheme. White America introduced a new and different type of slavery. It was designed to destroy all elements of the black family. History has no equal to match the terrible ways in which White America treated and destroyed the black family. White America stole it, but Black America must return it.

# What was the Black African Family's life like?

Most of the inhabitants on the beautiful sun-kissed land of Africa had strong family ties. The family would collectively care for the appropriate needs of its members. A man, woman, and child could find comfort in their family and from their family. Often, grandparents, parents, children and grandchildren all lived together. The grandparents received the highest respect and honor from the family members. It was through the grandparents that the children learned family history, folklore, and proverbs. The oldest male was usually the head of the family. The immediate and extended families cared for their widows, their sick, and their orphans. Family ties were firm.

The bride and groom had a wider union than that of just two people getting married. It united two families. As part of the marriage arrangements, frequently property was exchanged. Often, the groom had to pay a price for the bride. The payment was paid to the bride's family either in money, in livestock, or in service. It was a gesture of compensation for the loss of their daughter. The bride and groom participated in elaborate ceremonies. The whole mating and marriage activities were a colorful and artful experience. Marriages were not made or broken without family and community support. Relatively few marriages were broken.

Wars existed between families, between tribes, and between countries. The consequences were the same as with any other people. Captives were taken as in other wars. Sometimes these captives were made slaves. As in any war, people were killed. However, history does not show deliberate efforts to destroy the family concept of a total people as later seen in America.

White America had a different type of slavery experience awaiting many of the African inhabitants. From across the turbulent Atlantic Ocean, the quiet but imperialistic America stalked the docile motherland of Africa and delivered a decisive blow to her children. This blow would cause wounds which would ooze with pus for centuries. America would boldly violate its own stated creed in its treatment of the inhabitants stolen from Africa.

> The thief cometh not but for to steal, and to kill, and to destroy...
>
> St. John 10:10

# What did White America do to the Black Family?

To make a black African a slave, White America chose to destroy the black family unit. Human rights such as marriages, family privileges, parental and child relationships were taken from blacks. Blacks were not considered human beings. The buying and selling of slaves was as common as the buying and selling of horses and cattle. Family members were separated. Many never saw each other again. The great freedoms that the early white fathers of America fought and stood for were not applied to the black family.

# How did White America choose to destroy the Black Family?

The American pattern of family structure was strange to the slaves from Africa. These slaves were not allowed to continue their form of family structure, and they were not allowed to participate freely in the American system of family structure.

Marriages among slaves were not recognized and protected by law. Nevertheless, the slave owner would often choose husbands for the women and wives for the men. Often, the slave owner would mate husband and wife for breeding purposes. If the slave refused, he or she was beaten into submission.[1] Some slavemasters had breeding farms. Often, the slave owner mated slaves for marriage who had never seen or heard of each other before.

The wedding ceremony was a disgrace. The slaveowner would secure a broom. He would instruct a male and a female to jump over the broom. After they jumped over the broom, he would then declare them married.[2] Some slaves had many such marriages.

The husband could see his wife only as the slaveowner saw fit. Even if the slaveowner decided to whip the wife, the husband could do absolutely nothing without putting his own life in danger. If a young black man wished to see a young black woman, often it was not his mother or father that he had to ask, but the slavemaster. There were many cases in which an adult woman could not date the male of her choice without the slavemaster severely beating the woman. Frederick Douglass, a former slave, relates an incident where his aunt was found in the company of a black male without the slavemaster's permission.

> "Before he [slavemaster] commenced whipping Aunt Hester, he took her into the kitchen, and stripped her from neck to waist, leaving her neck, shoulders, and back, entirely naked. He then told her to cross her hands, caller her at the same time a d--d b--h. After crossing her hands, he tied them with a strong rope, and led her to a stool under a large hook in the joist, put in for the purpose. He made her get upon the stool, and tied her hands to the hooks. She now stood fair for his infernal purpose. Her arms were stretched up at their full length, so that she stood upon the ends of her toes.

> Then he said to her, "Now, you d--d b--h, I'll learn
> you how to disobey my orders!" and after rolling up
> his sleeves, he commenced to lay on the heavy
> cowskin, and soon the arm, red blood (amid heart-
> rending shrieks from her, and horrid oaths from
> him) came dripping to the floor. I was so terrified
> and horror-stricken at the sight, that I hid myself in
> a closet, and dared not to venture out till long after the
> bloody transaction was over."__

In some cases, incest occurred.[4] One account tells of how a mother had a child who was badly burned on the side of his face. This child had accidentally fallen into an open fire. This child was taken from his mother and sold at a very young age. Years later this mother was matched for marriage with a young man. Upon asking this young man how he received the burn on the side of his face, he stated that he received the burn when he accidentally fell from his mother's arms into open flames, and burned the side of his face. The mother then recognized that her husband was also her son. The mother then fainted.[5]

Many black children were born because the slave master forced the union of a black male and a black female. Many of the children were sold away from the father and the mother. Sometimes, when the children were taken to another plantation, some mothers who were able to find their children, killed the children and then committed suicide. Others, upon learning that their child would be sold away from them, killed the child and committed suicide. Many families were separated, never to see or hear of each other again.

Slaves were treated like animals and bred like cattle. To the slaveowner and White America, the black female was just a cow, the black male just a bull, and the black child just a calf. White America treated blacks as though they were insensitive to pain, fear, and loneliness.[6]

# Why did White America chose to destroy the Black Family?

"For the love of money is the root of all evil."

I Timothy 6:10

When the apostle Paul wrote this scripture, he must have looked down through the ages and seen White America. To satisfy her economic appetite, White America would do anything.

"Slavery has always been an evil institution, and
being a slave has always been undesirable. However,
the slave in America was systematically exploited
for the accumulation of wealth."[7]

Frequently any type of stable relationships was discouraged because White America felt that this would interfere with slave trade or human slave breeding. White America did not care about black relationships and feelings when it came to making money. Black America should never forget this. And if one looks closely at many service organizations, including some hospitals and even some church organizations, one will find often that economic gains determine the service - not need, not love, and not concern, when it comes to blacks.

An effective way to eliminate the family concept is to destroy the dignity of its components. Therefore, White America attacked the dignity of the fathers, the mothers, and the children of the Black Family.

An effective way to eliminate the family concept is to destroy the dignity of its components. Therefore, White America attacked the dignity of the fathers, the mothers, and the children of the Black Family.

# Chapter 3

# What Did White America Do to the Black Mother?

"Nobody knows de trouble I seen."

The slaves experienced a 'breaking-in-period.'[8] During this period, it was the purpose of the slaveowners to break the spirits of their captives and mold them into accepting the slaveowners' inhumane expectations.

To accomplish this, blacks were forced to watch some of the cruellest acts ever witnessed by mankind. One such act was a forced tieing of a naked black pregnant woman to a tree. The scared stares of her fellow slaves must have been pain to her mind. The sun that once soothed her must have been pain to her body. But the greatest pain of all must have been the sight of the white maniac, the slaveowner. For in his hand, was a large knife. This knife announced pain and death. The slaveowner would take the knife, plunge it into her abdomen, and cut her belly open. Then he would pull the unborn baby out of this dying mother and throw its helpless life to the ground.

This demonstration was performed, so that the women would

know that their bodies and their children belonged only to the slavemasters and that life and death were in his hands. It was an attempt to steal from the black woman her God given ability to birth her own child, her God given responsibility to take care of her own child and her God-given right to guide her own child by her own free wisdom.

These and other similar incidents created unimaginable fears. These fears were not just of suffering and death, but also of losing God's greatest gift to womanhood - motherhood.

To increase her mental torture, the black woman was not guaranteed the choice of who the father of her child would or would not be. The slavemaster would choose who would mate with whom, and his choice was usually determined by economic reasons. A former slave recalls:

> "My mother told me that he [her master] owned a woman who was the mother of several children, and when her babies would get about a year or two of age he'd sell them, and it would break her heart. She never got to keep them. When her fourth baby was born and was about two years old, she just studied all the time about how she would have to give it up, and one day she said, 'I just decided I'm not going to let Old Master sell this baby; he just ain't going to do it.' She got up and give it something out of a bottle and pretty soon it was dead."[9]

The slavemaster would force the slaves to breed, so he could sell the children. The black woman was valued by her ability to breed.

In his attemp to further stamp out personal dignity, the white man would also use the black woman for his own personal sexual sickness.[10] History shows that at one time there were as many as three hundred thousand babies, as a result of white men impregnating black slave women.[11] Remember, whenever a woman is forced to participate sexually without her consent, it is rape. White America institutionalized a system that raped millions of people. That reputation is unparaleled in history. White America - the Great Rapist. The black woman was raped and sexually exploited like no other woman in the history of mankind.

The black woman's sorrow, however, did not end with the sexual act. Besides being forced to perform sexually for the sick desires of the slavemaster at night, she had to work in the hot fields during the day. If a black woman resisted, frequently she was stripped naked, tied to a stake and beaten in the same manner that black men were beaten.[12]

In most cases, these women received no mercy. Even when the black mother was pregnant, she had to work in the fields. Almost immediately after childbirth, she was required to return to the fields. A former slave recalls:

> "As we went out in the morning, I observed several women, who carried their young children in their arms to the field. These mothers laid their children at the side of the fence, or under the shade of the cotton plants, whilst they were at work; and when the rest of us went to get water, they would go to give suck to their children, requesting someone to bring them water in gourds, which they were careful to carry to the field with them. One young woman did not, like the others, leave her child at the end of the row, but had contrived a sort of rude knapsack, made of a piece of coarse linen cloth, in which she fastened her child, which was very young, upon her back; and in this way carried it all day, and performed her task at the hoe with the other people."[13]

If these mothers stopped working for short periods of time to rest, and if they could not keep up with the other workers, they were severely beaten. About one out of every three black females gave birth to ten or more children.

Although White America tried everything possible to destroy the personal dignity of the black woman, and despite all these terrible experiences, the black woman survived. If greatness is defined as the ability to absorb more pain and indignity than others and still function, then the Black American Woman must be the greatest woman on earth. She should be declared as the queen of the earth. Maya Angelou's statement in describing the substance of the black woman deserves repeating, over and over and over again.

> "There is a kind of strength that is almost frightening in Black women. It's as if a steel rod runs right through the head down to the feet. And I believe that we have to thank Black women not only for keeping the Black family but the white family...Because Black women have nursed a nation of strangers. For hundreds of years, they literally nursed babies at their breasts who they knew, when they grew up, would rape their daughters and kill their sons."[16]

I am dark but lovely...

Song of Solomon 1:5

# Chapter 4

# What Did White America Do to the Black Father?

Blacks came from a country where many men were warriors and family heads. These black warriors and black family heads, however, offered a threat to White America's economic plans. But, these warriors and family heads, if made slaves, could bring the highest economic return for White America. Therefore, the submission of the black males became a major emphasis and resulted in the development of a new slave system — a slave system designed to destroy the manhood of the black males.

## How Did White America Destroy the Black Father?

About 15 million African captives were slated to become slaves in America. This group consisted of men, women, and children. These survivors saw about 5 out of every 100 slaves murdered on the shores of Africa, resisting slavery. Once on the slave ships, they witnessed the death of about 13 out of every 100 slaves either by suicide, disease, or murder by whites. During the first three months in the new world, they experienced the horrible sight of about 33 out of every 100 slaves murdered at the hands and commands of the slavemasters.[17] After witnessing such brutality, the survivors themselves had to endure a breaking-in-period and the milling process.

## The Milling Process

To change whole brown wheat grains into white flour, the manufacturer sends the grains through a milling or refining process. This process removes the fiber and the bran. Fiber and bran are very nutritious parts of the grain. This milling process also removes 90 percent of Vitamin B1 and 50 percent of the other 12 or so vitamins and minerals. The manufacturer replaces about 4 of these vitamins. Now when these 4 are replaced, the manufacturer then calls the flour or bread 'enriched.' In other words, it is like a person taking 12 dollars from you and giving back to you 4 dollars, and then saying he has enriched you. In reality, he has not enriched you. He has stolen from you.

White America had a milling experience awaiting the black male. Like other men of the world, the black male was created with a spiritual dimension, a physical dimension, a mental dimension, a social dimension, and a psychological dimension. Through the milling process of slavery, White America milled these dimensions in the black male and then replaced or 'enriched' some of these dimensions with inferior versions. The black male was milled and 'enriched' so that White America would be 'made rich.'

During this milling process, the black slave from Africa was not allowed to speak his native tongue or practice his native customs. The black males were constantly intimidated. Many times when the slavemaster received a new slave, he would have the new slave severely beaten. The purpose of this beating was to intimidate him so that the slave would give his best work production on his first day. For example, if the task was to pick cotton, the slavemaster would weigh the cotton at the end of the first day after the beating. That weight would serve as a standard for that slave. If he fell short of that weight, he was subject to be severely beaten again.[18]

Black males were beaten and tortured in many ways. Austin Steward, a former slave recalls:

> "The usual mode of punishing the poor slave was, to make them take off their clothes to the bare back, and then tie their hands before them with a rope, pass the end of the rope over the beam, and draw them up till they stood on the tips of their toes. Sometimes they tied their legs together and placed rail between. Thus prepared, the overseer proceeded to punish the poor, helpless victim. Thirty-nine was the number of lashes ordinarily inflicted for the most trifling offense.

> "Who can imagine a position more painful? Oh, who, with feelings of common humanity, could look quietly on such torture? Who could remain unmoved, to see a fellow-creature thus tied, unable to move or to raise a hand in his own defense; scourged on his bare back, with a cowhide, until the blood flows in streams from his quivering flesh? And for what? Often for the most trifling fault; and, as sometimes occurs, because a mere whim or caprice of his brutal overseer demands it. Pale with passion, his eyes flashing and his stalwart frame trembling with rage, like some volcano, just ready to belch forth its fiery contents, and in all its might and fury, spread death and destruction all around, he continues to wield the bloody lash on the broken flesh of the poor, pleading slave, until his arm grows weary, or he sinks down, utterly exhausted, on the very spot where already stand the pools of blood which his cruelty has drawn from the mangled body of his helpless victim, and within the hearing of those agonized groans and feeble cries of 'Oh do, Massa! Oh do, Massa! Do, Lord, have

> mercy! Oh, Lord, have mercy!'
>
> "Often, slaves were murdered just to set an example and to generate fear. The slaves received beatings if they said the wrong word, looked the wrong way or spoke too loudly at the slavemaster, looked dissatisfied, or made a mistake."[19]

Outside the regular whipping or floggings, White America would cut off ears, hands, and feet of the slaves. Occasionally they would strip a slave naked, force him or her to lie face down with arms and legs outstretched and tied to stakes. The slavemaster then would take a cat by the tail and rake it across the back of slave. The claws of the cat would rip the skin of the victim. It was a common occurrence for a slave to be tied by his hands hanging from the rafters for hours. A slave could be beaten with anything and for anything. If death happened in the process, it was just a loss of a slave. Frederick Douglass tells about the death of his wife's cousin.

> "She had been sent that night to Mrs. Hick's [a white woman] baby and during the night she fell asleep, and the baby cried. She, having lost her rest for several nights previous, did not hear the crying. They were both in the room with Mrs. Hicks. Mrs. Hicks, finding the girl slow to move, jumped from her bed, seized an oak stick of wood by the fireplace, and with it broke the girl's nose and breastbone, and thus ended her life.... Thus she [Mrs. Hicks] escaped not only punishment, but even the pain of being arraigned before a court for her horrid crime."[20]

White America milled the manhood of the black male slave and enriched him as a 'boy.' White America tortured and savagely treated the black male until White America turned these survivors from warriors and family heads to subdued human beings. White America made the black man into a 'boy.' A similar response was demonstated by captives in the Nazi concentration and extermination camps. After much stress, these inmates began to manifest childlike behavior.[21]

The black father had no legal marriage, no legal family, and no legal control over his children. The black male did not have complete choice of who his mate would be. Also, once a mate was chosen and a child was born, the black father did not have authority over his own child. White America took away the black male's role as father and husband. Therefore, responsibility, discipline, and direction for his family, including his children, were not in his hands... Not having the opportunity to dertermine destiny, eventually means that one will not. If not allowed to think, eventually one may not.

The black man was only a breeder. Parental authority was in the hands of the slavemaster. As a father, the black man was so humiliated that he was not looked upon as a father or a man. Slavery for the black males "prevented their coming to emotional maturity by inflicting on them a perpetual childhood, and imposing their master's ideology on them, resulted in their identifying themselves with their masters."[22]  The slave was the child and the slavemaster was the father.[23] In this boy role, the black male had to approach White America with bowed head. The black male had to answer with a 'yes suh, no suh.' And the slavemaster and White America called the black man, 'boy.' The slavery experience for the black man was perpetual childhood.

# Chapter 5

# What Did White America Do to Destroy the Black Child?

Sometimes I feel like a motherless child,
along ways from home,
along ways from home.

The child who does not have a childhood while he is a child can be more easily made into a child when he is an adult. During slavery, the black child was deprived of his childhood. A child without a childhood is a good candidate for becoming an adult 'boy' when he becomes a man.

## How Did White America Try to Destroy the Black Child?

White America tried to destroy the black child by destroying his childhood. After living nine months in the belly of a mother who was experiencing great stress and frustration daily, the black child was born into a system controlled by those who did not consider him a human being.

Most black slave children were born out of wedlock. Many did not know who their fathers were. The black child was the product primarily of either no father, a temporary father, a humiliated father, or a multiple father environment. Also, frequently the conception of the child was not out of a love between two human beings, but rather from a forced union of two people by the slavemaster. The slaveowner, who had power over the child's destiny, viewed black children as cattle - born as a result of breeding.

Black children suffered a high incidence of infant death. Some babies were beaten to death by the slaveowner's wife because she suspected that her white husband was the father of the child.

The black child was not assured of receiving the nurturing that babies need. Often, black mothers were forced to show more affection to the children of the slavemaster than to her own.

Mothers were usually required to return to the fields shortly after the child was born. If the child was allowed to go in the fields with the mother, he usually had to be left at the end of the field, while she kept up with the rest of the workers. Many black children received limited attention from their parents. Many black mothers had to return to the fields without their babies. Frederick Douglass, reports,

> "Frequently, before the child has reached its twelfth month, its mother is taken from it, and hired out on some farm a considerable distance off, and the child is placed under the care of an old woman, too old for field labor. For what this separation is done, I do not know, unless it be to hinder the development of the child's affection toward its mother, and to blunt and destroy the natural affection of the mother for the child."[24]

Black babies were often cared for by children who were not much older than the newborn babies themselves. As a form of punishment to the black mother, sometimes her black child was taken from her and sold on another plantation. These black children also saw White America commit rapes, unmerciful beatings, and other abuses upon their mothers and other black slave women. Frederick Douglass reports an experience he witnessed as a young slave child.

> "I have often been awakened at the dawn of day by the most heart-rending shrieks of an own aunt of mine, who he [slavemaster] used to tie up to a joist, and whip upon her naked back till she was literally covered with blood. No words, no tears, no prayers, from his gory victim, seemed to move his iron heart from its bloody purpose. The louder she screamed, the harder he whipped; and where the blood ran fastest, there he whipped longest. He would whip her to make her scream, and whip her to make her hush; and not until overcome by fatigue, would he cease to swing the blood-clotted cowskin. I remember the first time I ever witnessed this horrible exhibition. I was quite a child, but I well remember it. I never shall forget it whilst I remember anything. It was the first of a long series of such outrages, of which I was doomed to be a witness and a participant. It struck me with awful force. It was the blood-stained gate, the entrance to the hell of slavery, through which I was about to pass. It was a most terrible spectacle. I wish I could commit to paper the feeling with which I beheld it."[25]

To the slaveowner, the black child was not much different from the black adult, only smaller. At about the age of seven, children had to work alongside adults. They were expected to produce almost as much as adults. These children had very few free childhood experiences.[26] When the child became about twelve years old, he was often sent to the auction block for sale. As a child, the black slave was constantly trained for the black 'boy' adulthood.

One can easily see how these experiences could affect the self-concept of the black child.

# Chapter 6

# Blacks' Response to Slave Experience

## First Level

The slavery experience for blacks in America was very stressful. Some writers have tried to say that things were not all that bad for some slaves. Not so. Granted that every black may not have personally experienced savage beatings, killings, or rapes perpetuated by the slaveowners and White America, yet, all slaves knew about these cruel acts, they all witnessed some of these cruel acts, and they all knew that these terrible acts could happen to any of them at any time as well. They also knew very well that the laws of the United States would not protect the black slave from such inhumane treatment. Therefore, all slaves were mentally, socially, and psychologically affected by these acts. Case closed.

Forced to endure the severely stressful situation of America's slave system, the black slave had to find ways in which to cope. Generally, there are three levels from which human beings cope. In extremely stressful situations, human beings usually use one or a combination of these three coping levels. The first level of coping includes fighting, running, or compromising.

## Coping by Fighting

Many blacks resisted slavery on the shores of Africa. Some succeeded. Many died in battle. Others fought their captors on the slave ships. A few of these uprisings succeeded. In uprisings that were not successful, slaves were beaten, tortured, thrown over board, or murdered. Uprisings also broke out during the breaking-in period and on the plantations. Over three hundred such uprisings occurred. Most of the slaves who participated in these uprisings were either severely beaten, tortured, or murdered. Occasionally, White America used government troops to contain slave uprisings. The black slaves who fought for human rights and justice met with terrible beatings and even death. Therefore, fighting was not a successful coping mechanism for the black slave.

## Coping by Running

The black slave had very few places to run to. Blacks were easily spotted. With bulldogs and blood hounds, White America hunted runaway slaves. Sometimes slaves were so badly lacerated by dogs that they would bleed to death. The black slave could find but very few places of refuge.

> "Being a slave in a democracy, he [the black slave] was put outside of the bounds of society. Finally, because his slavery was racially defined, his plight was incurable. Although he might flee from slavery, he could not escape his race."[27]

> "Sucessful slave escapes were relatively rare, although attempted escapes were numerous. The absence of sheltered places of refuge, the vast

distances to be covered, the slave's ignorance of
geography, his illiteracy, isolation and general lack
of knowledge, plus his high visibility, were among
the reasons why escapes were so difficult. All the
more remarkable and heroic are the slaves who
succeded in escaping."[28]

In order to make it difficult for the slaves to run away,
slavemasters branded the slaves with red hot irons. White
America could easily identify a branded slave. The slavemasters
branded many slaves on the sides of their faces. On July 18,
1838, the North Carolina Standard newspaper carried this ad:

> "TWENTY DOLLARS REWARD. Runaway
> from the subscriber, a negro woman and two
> children; the woman is tall and black, a few days
> before she went off, I burnt her with a hot iron on
> the left side of her face; I tried to make the letter M,
> and she kept a cloth over her head and face, and a
> fly bonnet over her head, so as to cover the burn;
> her children are both boys, the oldest is in his
> seventh year; he is a mulatto and has blue eyes; the
> youngest is a black and is in his fifth year."

Some blacks chose to run away or to escape from the slavery
experience by committing suicide. Suicide was a common
occurrence. Slaves jumped overboard from the slave ship to their
deaths and suicide continued all through the slavery experience.

> Before I be a slave
> I be buried in my grave.

Running away was not a very successful way of coping for most
slaves.

## Coping by Compromise

The black slave did not have much opportunity for bargain-
ing, did not have much eligibility for human mercy, did not have
many occasions for human dignity, and therefore, did not have
much room for coping by compromise. Hence, coping by

fighting, by running, or by compromise was not very successful. In conclusion, these first levels of coping mechanism were not positive survival choices.

# Chapter 7

# Blacks' Response to the Slavery Experience

## Blacks' Response to the Slavery Experience Second Level

When Blacks could not successfully use the first levels of coping mechanisms for survival and human dignity, many turned to the second level. The second level includes the ego-defense mechanisms. These mechanisms are used to protect the person's self-concept. These ego-defense mechanisms protect the self from insults, psychological hurt, and disorganization. Ego-defense mechanisms are learned. Often, they become habitual. Sometimes they lead to a degree of self-deception and distortion of reality. Still, these defenses may help the person to maintain control and self-esteem. There are at least 10 ego-defense mechanisms, but only the major ones used by the black female, the black male, and White America will be mainly discussed. For the black female, the most common ego-defense was 'compensation.' The black male primarily used the ego-defense 'rationalization.' White America generally responded to slavery with the ego-defense, 'intellectualism.'

It is important to remember that for the black slave these defenses were survival choices. Their choices were the best under the circumstances and practical for the unique situation. These coping behaviors were practiced until they became a way of life for the slaves. Generally they were then passed down from one generation to another. Sons and daughters of slaves picked up these defenses and behaviors from their mothers and fathers. These sons and daughters grew up, and they passed these defenses and behaviors on to their children, and so on. Many of these characteristics still exist in the black family today although social environment and situations may cause some changes and modifications.

## The Black Female and Compensation

Compensation is a way of making up for something that is missing, or making up the difference. To destroy the black family, White America tried to eliminate the role of the black male as father. White America did however, allow the slave mother more flexibility with her children than they allowed the slave father with the children. Because of this, and because of the restriction placed upon the black man in the black family, the black woman had to compensate or make up the difference, and she did. She was the most stable and consistence element of the black family unit.

Often, the most powerful slave on the plantation was an older woman.[29] She was usually a grandmother. Often, she cared for the slavemaster's children and could say things to the slavemaster that other slaves, particularly black males, dare not say. White America made the black family a matriarchal unit — a family headed and controlled, although out of necessity, more often by the black woman than the black man.

Many black mothers had but a short time to nurture their children and to give their children specific directions for life.

Still, they had more control of these directions and could spend more time with their children than were allowed slave fathers.

Many black mothers assumed both mother and father roles. The black male's role as a father was unstable and unpredictable. Except as a breeder and a worker, it was hard to determine the black father's role. If the slave male was allowed his role as a father, it was controlled by the slaveowner and influenced by the black mother, and therefore, became a week role. Children could indentify their mothers more than they could identify their fathers.

The slave mother also saw that if her son was to survive the slavery experience, his chances were best if he was physically strong, a good breeder, and docile to White America. Often a black mother encouraged this type of behavior in her son. She prepared her son to someday be a good 'adult boy.' She encouraged his sexual masculinity. She beamed as she watched him grow strong. Yet, she was usually the first to whack him if he suggested a change in White America's slave system!

To prepare her son for a stable relationship was to set her son up for disappointment. This became the greatest dilemma for the black woman. Even today many black mothers are preparing their sons to be the type of men whose characteristics they despise in a mate. For example, how often does a black mother beam with pride and express how cute it is when her young son flirts with several girls at a time. How proudly she announces that her Leroy has two or three girl friends! What these mothers are doing is encouraging girl hopping. Even as late as the 1950's, one of the main characteristics for popularity among the teenage black males was the number of girls they had seduced. So when Leroy grows up and marries, some woman will have to contend with Leroy's well trained wishes for a fling with two or three or more women simultaneously. This same woman (Leroy's wife) who does not like this characteristic in Leroy will probably encourage this same characteristic in her own son.

To make things more complicated, Leroy's mother does not like, in Leroy's father, this same characteristic that she has encouraged in Leroy. At the same time, she thinks that Leroy's wife should be more tolerant of this same behavior in Leroy. Leroy's mother is quick to show that the daughter-in-law is probably the cause of Leroy's actions and reactions. Often, this mother will describe her son's irresponsible behavior as though it is 'cute.' Many black mothers are overprotective of their children, even against the fathers' authority. They often use and play the children against the father.

The female slave's relationship with the male slave was screened by a distant admiration. Her only chance of having any stable relationship with a particular black man was if the black man offered no threat to the evils of slavery. If he displayed any aggression against slavery, he was usually severely beaten, sold to another plantation, or killed. Therefore, many agressions by the black man were discouraged by the black woman. She did this to protect him. Consequently, many black women were conditioned to discourage certain aggressive behaviors in black men, particularly those behaviors that challenged or competed with White America. Even today, one of the most consistent types of husbands and fathers are the mansy-pansy types - fathers with a subdued authority that is well 'controlled' by the wishes of the mother.

"As is the mother, so is her daughter." Exekiel 16:44

## The Black Male and Rationalization

Sometimes a person encounters a situation where he must perform a particular act or behavior that is not really acceptable to his self-respect or conscience. He may cope with this situation by rationalization. To do this, he must form in his mind an acceptable reason for performing this act. He uses his own socially acceptable reason because the real reason damages his self-respect and self-concept. For example, a student who may not receive good grades in school may rationalize and say that the classes in school are for sissies, and, therefore, he is not interested in school. The real reason he does not like school is that he is not performing well. And when one does not perform well, one is looked down upon. Therefore, the poor student tries to take the focus off his performance and direct the problem to something else. He rationalizes that if school could reach his standard, then he could go for school. In reality, he does not perform well in school because he does not have the skills or does not apply himself to the necessary study.

The black male was not allowed the responsibility of total freedom to be father to his children and to be husband to his wife.

> "The 'real' father was virtually without authority over his child, since discipline, parental responsibility, and control of rewards and punishments all rested in other hands; the slave father could not even protect the mother of his children except by appealing directly to the master. Indeed, the mother's role loomed far larger for the slave child than did that of the father. She controlled those few activities — household care, preparation of food, and rearing of children — that were left to the slave family. For that matter, the very etiquette of plantation life removed even the honorific attributes of fatherhood from the Negro male, who was addressed as boy — until, when vigorous years of his prime were past, he was allowed to assume the title of uncle."[30]

Often, he was just a breeder. So, he rationalized and glorified this situation. He began to look at his situation as desirable. He began to brag about how many women he had impregnated and how many families he had fathered. The black slave male viewed himself as an unconfined stud. Many would not allow themselves to become attached to their families because it was too hurting when these family members were taken away and there was very little they could do about it.

As a result, many slave fathers became unattached to their children and families. Accepting this unattachment became a way of life. Therefore, young boys saw adult males unattached. They grew up and became unattached, or at least minimally attached. This life style was passed on from one generation to another. And so today, many black males are fathers of several families, but take little or no responsibility for their children. They may sometimes give money to the mother and the children, if money is available, but they do not offer much nurturing to their children. They have a hit-and-run philosophy and brag about this to their peers. They also feel that the marriage arrangement is too confining.

Male slave adults found comfort in hanging out with other male slave adults, talking and rapping. These rapping sessions became the outlet or the sounding board for rationalizing. This style has been passed onto the present generation. For example, just go down any main street in the black community and you will find men, old and young, hanging out, rationalizing. Frequently when a lady passes by one of these gatherings, there is at least one male from the group who must demostrate that he has the charm to sexually challenge the lady. Sometimes he may walk a short ways from the group to get a better look at the lady. He may make a comment like, "Baby you sure look good!" He may make a gesture and sometimes fall into his cool walk. He then returns to the group and waits for some comments of approval from the group. If a lady passes that he knows, he sometimes calls the lady over, away from the group, and secretly whispers a few words to her (usually about nothing). He returns to the group hoping that someone will say something like "Man, that must be one of your ole ladies." His ego has been satisfied. Jacqueline Hokes-Neal, a talented musician and song writer, observed the life-styles of a group of black men in the Summer of '84.' She summarized her observations and thoughts in her song "Black Man." (See Appendix A.)

The black male still prides himself as a breeder. He loves to brag about being a father without having the responsibility of being a husband. The pressure is high, even today, on young black males to establish themselves as potential breeders. As a young man, being a potential breeder gives him respect and acceptance with his friends and age group. I remember one situation in which a young teenager kept a condom (rubber) on his penis for several hours so he could show his friends that he had had sexual intercourse with a young woman.

## White America and Intellectualism

The ego-defense of intellectualism can be used to relieve the person's conscience of guilt. Usually, this guilt is relieved by bias logic. By accepting, promoting, and allowing its slavery system, America violated its Christian religion, its country's creed, and its human dignity. Therefore, to relieve the guilt, White America had to believe that the American slavery system was God's will, and that blacks were not human beings.

America was established on the concept of freedom, equality, and justice for all human beings. The slavery system however, created some real problems for America. She had to do something to relieve her hypocrisy and guilt. Her honest conscience stated that

> "America is a country which promotes freedom
> and justice for all human beings. Blacks are human
> beings. Therefore, blacks are entitled to freedom
> and justice."

But, White America had developed this savage, ruthless system of slavery. So, to appease its conscience, White America developed an 'intellectual' defense. It stated

> "America is a country which promotes freedom
> and justice for all human beings. We do not allow
> freedom and justice for the black slave. Therefore,
> blacks slaves are not human beings."

Hence, White America talked about slaves as though they were less than human. Slaves were not protected by the law established for the human family in America.

Other 'logic' went like this:

> "We are a Christian nation. We, as a nation, have black slaves. Therefore, it is God's will that Christian nations have black slaves."

When White America came to this country of the Native Americans (Indians) and established America, they proclaimed this nation a Christian country, and ratified the Constitution and its laws in God's name. America proudly announced 'In God We Trust'. America - a haven for all people. America - a Christian nation. But, then slavery appeared, and White America searched the Bible for justification for their savage act. White America wrote books and articles trying to justify their heinous crimes against blacks. They proclaimed that slavery was the 'will of God.' A former slave reports:

> "I have said my master found religious sanction for his cruelty. As an example, I will state one of many facts going to prove the charge. I have seen him tie up a lame young woman, and whip her with a heavy cowskin upon her naked shoulders, causing the warm red blood to drip; and, in justification of the bloody deed, he would quote this passage of Scripture — 'He that knoweth his master's will, and doeth it not, shall be beaten with many stripes.'

> "Master would keep this lacerated youuung woman tied up in this horrid situation four or five hours at a time. I have known him to tie her up early in the morning, and whip her before breakfast; leave her, go to the store, return at dinner, and whip her again, cutting her in the places already made raw with his cruel lash."[31]

White America still feels that way today. If you listen to the white hatred groups, including the Klu Klux Klan, you can still hear this tune being whistled. They pronounce their actions as the 'will of God.'

There is also a more subtle voice that you must listen closely to. This voice is from the so-called 'conservative Christian group' which says,

> "We need to get our country back to those things
> that made us great as a Christian nation."

That sounds good. But, one must wonder, whether they are talking about Biblical principles or slavery concepts. Remember that when America was at its height as a Christian nation, so was black slavery at its height in America. Also remember that White America interprets Biblical principles through economic greed. When these so called Christian leaders speak of and have more economic concerns for the Aparthied government in South Africa than human rights for the oppressed people of that country, then we know that the slavemaster mentality is alive in America and in high places. And not all are necessarily wearing sheets over their heads.

One way in which to counter this ego-defense 'intellectualism' in White America is to make public every racial atrocity possible. The method of intellectualism is used to keep White America looking clean. She must be exposed. There are enough good Americans (white, black, yellow and red) who will rise against the monster when she is truly exposed.

# SUB-SECTION

# EGO-DEFENSE BLASTING

One of the best ways in which to deal with the ego-defense mechanism and its responses is direct confrontation, relationship building, and constant practice of the proper behavior. The black family members must face these problems directly and make the necessary changes that will build strong black families. These changes can happen through effective planning and consistent execution of those plans. Black slaves did not have the freedom to plan for themselves or for their families. Without the freedom to plan, blacks had limited control over their destiny and direction. Lack of planning allows one to be always controlled by the present situation. And the situation for blacks in America has not been and is not good.

# Chapter 8

# Relationship Development Plan

The black woman was the strongest and the most stabilizing factor in the black family during slavery. Since slavery, tradition has allowed her much the same role. Those coping defenses, which were once necessary, now work against the total building up of the black family. The black woman, with her strengths, must play a key role in making the black family all that it can be. She must use her power and energy along with the black male to reestablish the black family.

The slavery experience caused a subtle hostility between the black male adult and the black female adult. This hostility continues to exist today. The black female adult plays the dominant role in the family, tries to maintain that role, but shows hostility because she does. The black male adult is raised and influenced by his mother's somewhat hostile concept of the black adult male. He finds himself fighting between his mother's influence, his mate's expectation, and his own aspiration. This situation can leave him very frustrated.

> "Wives, submit yourselves unto your own husbands,
> as unto the Lord. For the husband is the head of the
> wife, even as Christ is the head of the church: and
> he is the saviour of the body."
>
> Ephesians 5:22,23

The mother and the wife need to support the husband as the father and the priest of his home. They should teach their children to respect their father as priest and head of his home. God, the Creator of mankind, designed it that way.

Since the black male has been damaged most and since the black female has also been the perpetuator of the male's fate (out of necessity and not willfully), she must be a key person in reestablishing the black father's role in the family. Traditionally, many black women discourage adventurous black men. Like the white society, many black women think that black men are not supposed to compete aggressively with society in areas other than sex and sports. This is because White America used the black male primarily as a breeder and steady physical worker.

The black woman and mother must encourage and support the black male to take leadership roles in all segments of the American society. If other Americans can enter, then no area should be taboo to black men. With support and confidence, the black wife must encourage her black husband. Trying to discourage him from the slavery 'boy' role by nagging him does not work. It only encourages him to hit-and-run and hang out.

> "Better to live alone in the desert than with a
> nagging and ill-tempered wife."
>
> Proverbs 21:19

> "Better to live in the corner of the house-top than
> have a nagging wife and brawling household."
>
> Proverbs 21:9

Some black women have been hurt and may be resentful in supporting the priest role of the father and husband. The black family cannot afford to continue this resentment. This resentment did not generate from the black man or the black woman. White America is responsible. This resentment developed during the slavery experience and has been passed down through generations. But now things must be turned around.

In many situations, the black woman will have to take the initiative in establishing the father's priest role. She must do what perhaps his mother did not do. Most black mothers did not train their sons to some day be priests of their families, but to be adult 'boys.'

The black woman must be patient and gentle. She must use that great strength, and energy that she has manifested over the centuries. She must use her strengths not only to maintain the family, she must use her energies not only to keep the family surviving, but also to build the priest role of the father. The black male will have no match once his energy and resources, which have been resisted and contained for centuries, have been released. Help make his day. Support him.

> "Husbands, love your wives, even as Christ also
> loved the church, and gave himself for it."
> Ephesians 5:25

In building the relationship, the husband must view the wife as his personal sacred being. He must see her as his special jewel, hewn especially for him. She is his unique helpmate. He must love her, he must protect her, he must care for her, and he must be willing to give his whole self for her. This means accepting her as he accepts himself. This means providing an environment of comfort for her. This also means protecting her from the outside influences that tear down the sacredness of the family — influences even from acquaintances and friends that damage the family relationship. To hurt her is to hurt himself. To abandon her is to abandon himself. He is her protector and a source of strength. To do less makes him less than a man.

The black male must perceive his family as his personal sacred unit. To allow his family to fall apart shows a failure somewhere. The black male who gives his commitment by the marriage vow, who without unreconcilable causes abandons his wife and family, may be just a boy still affected by the slavery experience. He has not matured to the awareness that relationships have to be nurtured and endured. Marriage is not an arena for boys. If he does not have the substance to take leadership and responsibility in his home, then he should wait until he is mature enough to do so. To continue to be a breeder, and not take financial and emotional responsibility for his family shows immaturity and although he may be 18 or 45, he is still a 'boy.' Children are not toys to be admired from a distance, but human beings who need nurturing and comfort in close and positive relationships. This includes the father's involvement.

As priest and leader of his home, he must take charge and direct the members of his family to their highest potential. The father's role as priest in his home is not one of dictatorship. A priest oversees, but he also serves and ministers to his family. The father role is to protect his family and to develop, provide, and maintain the opportunity for physical, mental, social, and spiritual growth for his family. Husband and wife must guard against those slavery responses that break down the black family.

# The self-fulfilling prophecy

If you treat someone like you expect him or her to be, it will influence and encourage that person to be that way. Studies on this concept, called the 'self-fulfilling prophecy, have proven this. Therefore, if the mother and children expect, respect, and treat the father and husband as priest and head of the home, he is more apt to take on this role. If they expect and treat the father and husband as a 'boy,' then he is more apt to hit-and-run. Also, if the husband expects, respects, and treats the mother and wife like the queen of the home and his special gift, then she is more likely to feel and respond like a queen. On the other hand, if he acts and performs like a slave boy - with limited responsibility and authority - then he will be perceived that way, and she will take on the role of protector. As protector, the mother and wife becomes overprotective of her children, even with her husband. This protector role causes subtle and sometimes aggressive hostility between the husband and wife. So the black husband and black wife must view each other in the positive role of priest and queen at all times, whether alone, with children, with friends, and other public occasions.

## Respect

During the slavery experience the roles of the family members were damaged, and, therefore, some respect for these roles was lost. Black husbands and wives must respect each other. We should also teach our children to respect the elderly. Children should have a special love and respect for their grandparents. Teach them to respect their parents. They should have special respect for their aunts and uncles. Teach them to value a system. Your family is a system. Teach them to respect God the Creator and respect the church. These values will help your children better relate to other systems in the society.

## Communication

Because the black slave was not allowed to participate in the American communication system of free expression, the slave developed his own. So, Black Americans have their own flavor of communication. Their verbal expressions are generally more emotional. They communicate through touch and gestures more than most Caucasian Americans. Their communications can be very colorful and sometimes ritualistic.

However, slavery has left some communication defects. In intimate relationships like marriage, the black male and the black female today seem to have a barrier in resolving differences verbally. Part of this evolved from the slavery experience. 'Telling each other off' became an outlet for frustrations. 'Telling each other off' also drew attention from other slaves.

Onlookers seemed to enjoy the conflict. Since relationships among the slaves were unstable anyway, 'telling someone off' mattered very little.

'Telling someone off' still has its attractive aspect. It is common today to see two parties come to the table of conflict to 'tell each other off' rather than resolve their differences. Unfortunately, often this 'telling off' technique is carried over into intimate relations, such as marriage. 'Telling someone off' does not build relationships. It creates barriers. Barriers will destroy intimate relationships. In a marriage, the 'telling somebody off' technique has to go.

To overcome this 'telling somebody off' technique, come to the arena of conflict with the purpose to resolve the differences. It is helpful to express that purpose to the person involved. Then the focus of conversation should be on the issue or situation that causes the conflict, not on the person. After you have discussed the issue or situation, then in respectful tones, express how this conflict affects you. Then talk about how to avoid such conflict in the future.

## Creativity Can Build Relationships

The husband should set aside 15 minutes each day to think and meditate on what can he can do that day to make his wife feel like the queen of their family. He should try to make the words, acts, or gestures different as much as possible. The black woman has taken on the role of queen in the black family for several hundred years. However, she needs encouragement. Encouraging her queenship in the family could include:

> occasionally bringing her flowers,
> telling her how much she means to him,
> stating how nice she looks,
> taking a walk together after supper,
> writing her little love notes
> exchanging duties (occasionally washing dishes &
> etc),

> taking her out to dinner
> spending private time together
> remembering special dates (birthdays,
>     anniversaries, holidays)
> etc,
> etc,
> and etc.

The couple should be creative. Both husband and wife should invest in a calendar and appointment book. They should plan times for activities similar to those mentioned above and write the activity, the date, and the time in their appointment books. If they do not plan for some things, they are not apt to do them.

The role of priesthood in the black family has been damaged. The husband needs to take some time and plan how, as priest, he could best serve his family. As priest of his home, he should determine his leadership roles in addressing his family's physical needs, their emotional needs, their social needs, and their spiritual needs.

Many black wives use their influence over the children as a method of getting revenge or fighting the father. They try to present, to the children, the worst image possible of the children's father. Often, when angry with their husbands, many mothers will persuade their children to side with them against their husbands. Sometimes this persuasion is very subtle. Many black mothers have mastered this technique. This is a terrible mistake. Not only does it destroy the priesthood image of the father to his children, but it educates the children to go into relationships with biases and hangups. Because of a sour relationship with their husbands, many black mothers have educated their daughters to a low expectation of marriage relationships. Therefore, they perpetuate the self-fulfilling prophecy. To the children, it is important that the wife and husband be supported to the roles of priest and queen even during times of conflict and difficulty, as well as times of happiness. Not only in the presence of the children should these roles be supported, but also with friends, other family members, and the public.

Husbands and wives who do not support each others' roles violate the relationship. Those that witness the violation of the relationship usually do not respect the relationship as much as before the violation. Some things are sacred to the family and should stay with family members only. This does not mean they should not talk with friends about family difficulties. It does mean, however, that they should only talk to them about issues and acts, not relationships. The priesthood and the queenship roles are sacred to the family and that sacredness must be maintained.

The wife should also set aside 15 minutes each day to think and meditate on what she can do that day to make her husband feel like priest of his family. She should try to make the words, acts, or gestures differ as much as possible. The black husband's confidence as priest has been damaged, therefore, much building is needed in this area. He must be encouraged to see and feel that his kingdom is his home and family and not the streets. His main responsibility is his home and family. She should encourage him in his role as priest, but not nag him about his role as priest. If she does, he, as many black men do, may freeze on her and tune her out. Black men have a way of easily doing that. The wife should learn how to communicate with him effectively. His priesthood should be encouraged by including his input on all major decisions for the family. Let him know and feel that as priest of his home, he has input in those decisions. She should teach her children to do the same. She should be creative.

## Sensitivity

It is highly likely that many black males have experienced nagging either from their mothers, their mothers nagging their fathers, or a nagging wife. Most black males have learned how to turn a deaf ear to the nagging female voice. With the deaf ear, comes a loss of sensitivity. However, to be effective with women, sensitivity is a must. The black male must learn to listen and feel the total needs of his mate. The black wife must also learn that nagging dulls sensitivity.

Black family members were separated during slavery. They must return to the immediate and extended family. They should not have parents, grandparents, or great-grandparents admitted to a nursing homes unless it is medically necessary. They need to have an extended family plan. The children should get together and determine how they will take care of mother, father, and grandparents when they are no longer able to take care of themselves. If a nephew or niece loses his or her parents, the extended family should take that family member in. Slavery should not be perpetuated by having this child tossed to and fro among strangers. The child should be taken in by his or her own blood. The family members should care for the child as they would their own. After all, he or she is.

# Trust

Without trust, no relationship is safe.Trust assumes consistency and loyalty. White America discouraged loyalty among slaves. White America also created as much inconsistency as possible to intimate slave relationships. It served White America's purpose well if slaves had a weak system of trust.

Black husbands and wives must learn to trust each other. The black man's reputation of hit-and-run has created an atmosphere of uneasiness among the black women. Uneasiness and suspicion hinder growth in a relationship. The hit-and-run technique of the black male is usually a response to insecurity. Black husbands and wives need to display trust. Trust and confidence will generate honesty and commitment more often than will distrust and suspicion. A healthy relationship must allow some independent space for both persons.

# Chapter 9

# Education Plan

"Take fast hold of instruction; let her not go; keep her, for she is thy life."

Proverbs 4:13

Parents are primarily responsible for their children. Providing educational opportunities is part of that responsibility. This responsibility and opportunity was denied the black slave. During slavery, it was against the law to even teach slaves to read or write. White America, in subtle ways, continues to make educational experiences difficult for many blacks.

In America today, ninety-two percent of white children are functionally literate, whereas, with black children, this number is fifty-eight percent. Rochester, New York, is a rather sophisticated city with comparatively high academic standards. However, out of 700 black high school graduates in 1985, only 23 had a 'B' average or better. In California in 1983, of 23,000 blacks that graduated from high school, only 838 met the requirements to enter the University of California. This type of poor performance by black children should not be and must not continue. Each black family needs to develop an educational plan.

This plan should start before the child is born. A child's home atmosphere and surroundings are his first school. Parents should prepare for him. They need to look closely at their homes. They should assess their educational attitudes and look at their ambitions and aspirations. Then they should ask themselves the questions: Is our home conducive to positive educational experiences for our child? Do we have positive educational attitudes, or are we locked into our own lack of educational achievements? Does our conversation smell with the stink of 'we cannot do,' rather than the perfume of 'we can do.' Parents must think and act positively so that these basic traits of ambition and achievements may be picked up by the child as he receives his first educational experience — the home.

When the child is born, parents should read to him daily. Many mothers make the mistake of sitting hours in front of the television, holding their babies while they watch soap operas. They are educating their babies to the idiot box (TV) though they do not understand what is going on. A better experience for the child would be reading, interacting, and talking to him. Furthermore, the radiation from that television is more harmful to the child than it is to the adult, especially if he is closer than 10 feet.

When the child gets a little older, many black mothers use the TV as a baby sitter. Hence, blacks spend more hours watching TV than whites. This precious time should be spent on reading and creative activities, and on active learning. Television is passive learning. The average black family watches TV about 6 hours a day. What a waste! A good investment, and a substitute for TV, is an educational computer, such as an Apple Computer. This can help him in much of his educational subjects, besides, children like to work on computers. The computer, however, should not to be a substitute baby sitter. The whole family can enjoy the computer together. Mom and Dad can also increase their educational experiences with the Apple Computer. High school, college courses, and college degrees can be gained through the computer. If the parents are involved in an educational or self-enrichment experience, this helps to develop a stronger educational atmosphere in the home. Many black parents can use some educational and self-enrichment experiences. Let us face it, blacks have some catching up to do, in some areas almost 300 years worth.

The mother and father are responsible for their children getting the necessary educational experience. Therefore, they should not depend solely on the school system to educate their children. They should take the time to find out how their children are doing daily. They should talk to them about their school experiences. They should encourage them to study for life, not just for a specific class. Special studying times in the home should be arranged. During this time, the parents should support the children by insisting that the home be quiet. The child should be taught to develop a regular pattern of studying, whether he has homework or not. Parents should visit the school at least twice a year and find out how the child is doing. Also, they should join the Parent Teacher Association (PTA).

The child should not be taught to look for educational handouts. Teach him to master the class subject, not to master methods of how 'to get by' in school. Many black parents encourage their children to settle for the least, while the child should be taught to settle for only the best. If the child is given a grade that he did not earn, he has settled for the least, even if the grade is an 'A'. If a child has worked hard, read his subject with interest, and can truthfully say in heart that he has given it his all, then he has settled for the best, even though he receives a 'C' for a grade. A parent should not depend on the teacher or the school to motivate the child to learn. Learning comes from within, not from without.

The child should be taught that there are many things in life that he will have to do that he is not going to like. That's life. The parent should tell him, however, that whether he likes them or not, if he has to do them, he must master them. If he takes this attitude into school, he will be a successful student. Many students who did not like a particular subject, enjoyed the subject after mastering it. A good practice for this concept is for the parent to assign him a variety of chores around the house - chores that he likes and chores that he dislikes. This will teach him to be a conquerer.

Black children must learn the importance of learning how to think. What children sow and deposit in their minds is what they will reap from their minds. If children spend 4 or 5 hours a day listening to music and watching television, then the quality of that music and the substance of those T.V. shows are the substance of their minds. Furthermore, White America used to perpetuate slavery concepts through biased text books. Now they do it more subtly through television.

Black radio stations are an important medium for education to the black youth. Many of the black youths spend a lot of time listening to black radio stations. Black youths are more than just a music receptacle with strong shoulders designed to carry music boxes. Black stations should include some educational programming for youth. Black radio stations should have a moral responsibility to black youth. Many of the lyrics to the music, educate youth to those loose morals that White America forced upon the slaves. Much of the music promotes sexual involvement without the responsibility of marriage. Blacks have enough unwed mothers. Parents, churches, and community groups should persuade black radio stations to exclude music that suggests loose morals. White America has done enough damage to black youth and families. Black musicians, black record companies, and black radio stations do not need to pick-up where White America left-off in damaging the family.

Education pays, but it also costs. Therefore, before the child is born, parents should start a bank account for his higher education. Into this education account at least $10 a week should be put. By the time the child finishes high school, enough will have been saved to give him a good financial start in college. Grants, loans, and handouts should not be counted on. If they are available, by all means parents and students should use them. But, they may not be there when it is time for the young child to enter college. Parents should do some research themselves on the educational opportunity for higher education (college). This should start as soon as the child enters high school. The child should be encouraged to do the same. If the child is not capable of researching this himself, then maybe he is not prepared for college.

Parents should teach their children or provide opportunities for them to learn how to communicate effectively. It is important that they concentrate on verbal skills. This was denied blacks. Language was taken from the slaves and an inferior version of English was forced upon them by mainly ignorant whites. Slaves were oriented to tones and gestures more than English grammar. In many situations, the tone of the slave's response determined whether he would be beaten. Not having the freedom to express himself left the slave to tone outlets and undertones. Blacks had to develop a completely different way of communication — a communication where English grammar was unimportant. Blacks are still very tone and gesture oriented when it comes to communication. Rapping is a rhythmic and tone oriented outlet of black expression. It is a work of art and nothing is wrong with it. But, black youth must also master the English language. It is the language of the marketplace. To have the freedom of expansion and growth, they must master the English language.

They should also develop an extensive vocabulary. Speaking of vocabularies, there are some words we need to exclude. One such word is 'nigger.' Nigger was a name given to black slaves by racist White America.

> "Africans were taught that Whites were superior to
> Blacks; that education, aspiration, even family life
> was for white people – not black people. Most

> important of these teachings was that the white man was master and had absolute power over All — black men, black women, and even white women. Seasoning was to transform the African to a slave, a brute, or a nigger (or nigress as the women were called). No name. No country. No religion. No achievements. No spouse. This was a nigger — a seasoned African who had broken all ties with Africa."[32]

Like other concepts of slavery, the white man started calling blacks 'niggers' and blacks picked up and continued it. Blacks called themselves 'niggers' because it was not as painful when they called themselves 'nigger.' That is how blacks were able to live with the word. At first, the word 'nigger' hurt. Today, blacks use the word so often, that it is sometimes used almost affectionately when blacks are referring to blacks. Some blacks enjoy using the word around white folks. Blacks should eliminate 'nigger' from their vocabulary. That name represents the slavery experience and blacks do not need a constant reminder.

According to the Bible, people of the black race are the descendants of Noah's son Ham. These descendants included the Egyptians, the Sumarians, the Canaanites, the Hittites, the Phoenicians and a host of other African people. These were the first builders of great cities and empires. They were the first cultivators of the world's food crops. They developed the first systems of trade, banking, commerce, mathematics, architecture and the science of building, and alphabet writing. Learning was a natural part of the black experience. Blacks were the first great masters of the world. They were master craftsmen and builders. However, the ingenuity of the black race has laid dormant for centuries. But, it must start again, and it can be rejuvinated. Writing and mathematics belonged to blacks and can belong again if black families are willing to apply themselves.

Black children must be trained to use both their minds and their hands. Blacks should get back to teaching their children a craft. Whether they shall be doctors, lawyers, teachers, or computer operators,they should still learn a craft or a trade, such as masonry, carpentry, cooking, auto mechanic or other trades. It is the mother's and father's responsibility to assure that this happens. There is nothing better than passing on crafts to children. Blacks should regain their gifts as master craftsmen and craftswomen.

It is very encouraging to see many black mothers (wed and unwed) going back after many years of absence to get their high school diplomas and in many cases getting college degrees. Everyone, no matter how old, should continually educate oneself. White America has tried to withhold this experience ever since they brought blacks here. Blacks must be hungry for education, hungry for learning. The statistics show that blacks have not been hungry for education but just participation. Black children have the same potential as any children on earth. However, this is not reflected when we look at the statistics. This is because the slavery experience killed the hunger for a broader educational experience. However, now is the time to re-kindle this hunger.

Educational experiences have not ment to many blacks what they should. The school has been used as a social and political football. We should stop allowing the state, the school board, and the politicians to do this to our children. Even some of our black social agencies have perpetuated social politics with children in school. The school should be there for no other reason except to educate the children. The main purpose of education is to prepare a child for life. The parents are the main persons responsible for this. Education is a total process and the public school system is only a part, not the whole. An important part of the education process is the family. We must not forget that the family is still the most important unit in the society.

# Chapter 10
# Sexual Plan

Sexual exploitation was one of the major areas of damage to the black family by the slavery experience. The parents should develop a sexual plan for their family before the children are born. Many of the sexual habits of blacks today are a direct result of the slavery experience and it is time for blacks to stop acting like slaves and wake up. Something is wrong. For example: More than one-half of black babies are born to unwed mothers.

White America forced the black slave woman into sexual activities for his personal greed. He, along with other white men of his choosing, and black male breeders that he chose, sexually damaged the dignity of the black woman. The black woman was not assured of any free commitment and responsibility from any of these groups. The sacredness of the black woman as a sexual being was greatly exploited. Many young black girls today are still affected by that slavery experience. Their sexual being is not sacred to them. They think that if they are old enough to bleed, then they are old enough to be butchered.

Black slave men also lost an appreciation for the sacredness of the sexual experience. White America made him a breeder and many remain that way today.

Parents can make a difference. They should start respecting the sacredness of the sexual experience and demonstrating that the sexual experience is a privilege for those that are committed by marriage. From a very early age, sons and daughters should be taught this concept. With sex comes responsibility. Therefore, no sex should be engaged in until they are ready for the responsibility. In other words, this means sex after marriage. Early dating by children is not wise. Parents should let children be children and give them time to develop before allowing them to have adult experiences. A young plant that is exposed to too much sun at too early an age gets burned and becomes dwarfed. Our children must know that certain kinds of pre-sexual behaviors can interfere with healthy families later.

Mothers and fathers must educate their young ladies to demand signs of responsibility from young men. Parents do not help young ladies and do not encourage responsibility in young men when they do not demand responsibility first. In other words, work before you eat. Fathers must educate prospective sons-in-law to "If you really want my daughter, then demonstrate that you are able and willing to marry her." If his intentions are otherwise, then he need not hang around.

Prostitution has existed for centuries, but the American 'pimp' concept was introduced by the slavemaster during the slavery experience in America. The slaveowner would force black female slaves to give their sacred bodies for his economic gain. If they refused, they were beaten severely. The white man taught some blacks very well how to continue slave concepts. Today, the demon is a different color, but he is just as ruthless. "Pimping is nothing more than the exploitation of Black womanhood in the crudest fashion."[33] The pimp can be seen in his big car, big hat, flashy coat, and ring-filled fingers, as he parades in the black communities sexually exploiting young confused girls.  These females have lost a sense of the sacredness of their bodies. They have lost their self-esteem, their pride, and their self-worth. They have returned to slavery. What a shame and what a waste!

> "The wise shall inherit glory; but shame shall be the promotion of fools."
>
> Proverbs 3:35

Parents must guard their daughters against the pimp and teach them to respect herself and teach her to demand respect. The pimp is the same scum as the slavemasters. Both destroy human dignity for money. Pimps are a constant reminder of what White America did to the black family. A pimp should be recognized as an enemy to the black family structure. Parents, local black churches, and politicians should combine efforts to eradicate such disease from the black neighborhoods. Remove this pollution from the influences of black children. It was bad enough when White America did this human degradation to black females, but to have black men continue this is sick.

# Chapter 11
# Family Enrichment Plan

At least once a month a specific day should be designated as family day. This is a time in which all family members get together to enjoy each other. Family members should have at least one meal together daily. Situations where people work or go to school may make it difficult, but the evening meal together could happen if there is effective planning. The time around the table should be sacred to the family and very pleasant, a time in which affections are shared, a time of relaxation, a time of comfort. The mother may have as much responsibility outside the home as others in the family. If mother works, then all the family should help to make a family evening meal possible. Things should be done together as a family.

The husband and wife need to develop a social plan for the child. They should consider: 'How are we going to integrate the child in the social process so that he will be a well rounded social being? When should this be an individualized experience and when should it be a group thing?' They should not just let things happen, but make things happen.

Blacks were not allowed to have a variety of experiences. Even today many limit their children and family to certain experiences. They are encouraged to think that certain experiences do not belong to black folk as they do to other Americans. Parents should plan and participate in museum trips and other activities so their children will grow up with a wealth of choices. This exposure should be the responsibility of the parents. If the experience is new to the parents, then they should take time to read up on it. They should look up the history of the event and know what to expect and then educate their child on it, or assign a responsible member of the family to do this. It should be an interesting learning experience for parents and family. Broadening horizons and exposing the family to a variety of new experiences is important, so they will be well exposed to America and its activities. A parent must be creative.

# Chapter 12
# Time and Space Plan

## Time

Time is an important resource. Unlike the privileged whites, the black slave was not allowed to use time to further his progress and growth. The black slave was deprived of both time and economics. By not having any control over his personal time, the black slave lost his sense of time. He would wait until the last possible minute before he would go out into the slavemaster's fields... After all, what human being would want to get up early in the morning and go on a job where he would received no appreciation or reward? Therefore, many blacks reacted against work and events by not respecting time.

Many black slaves also lost their appreciation of time. Some welcomed old age, some welcomed death. Many were looking forward to that 'time' after death — a 'time' of no more sorrows, no tears, and no more deaths.' These feelings of that better time was strongly expressed in the Negro spirituals.

Even today, blacks do not usually start their meetings on time. Often, it is heard, "I'm not going early, you know we're not going to start on time." However, to be effective, blacks must learn to master time. Time and economics go hand in hand.

Time is also associated with progress. When referring to progress for blacks, Americans have often expressed "now is not quite the time." During the '84' presidential campaign, the following radio jingle for Jessie Jackson somewhat articulated the American 'time' problem with blacks and progress:

> It's incredible!
> That blacks have been in America for over 300
>      hundred years and are still not classified as first
>      class citizens.
> It's incredible!
> That Europeans can come to America and be
>      treated as first class even before they become
>      citizens.
> Its incredible!
> That blacks are constantly told that now is not the
>      time — not the time for integration, not the time
> for equal jobs opportunities, not the time for equal
> housing, not the time for this and not the time for
> that.
>
> It's incredible!
> That when Jessie Jackson decided to run for
>      President, they cried 'now is not the time'...And
>      even some blacks whistle that tune.
> Now, that's incredible!
> Folks, let's stop this incredible nonsense and do
>      something credible. Get out, vote, and determine
>      your own destiny.

Blacks must master the sense of time, the appreciation of time, time and economics, and time and progress.

# Space

White America would not allow the black slave to have his

own space. He was forced to live in shacks. He was not allowed to own property. Many slaves lost their appreciation for property.

Even after slavery, America deprived blacks from the freedom of space. The spaces accessible to blacks were usually dirty, stinky, and filthy. Blacks would use these properties to lease their necessities but these experiences were surely not conducive for appreciation of space and property. As an ego-defense, many slaves lost their sense of appreciation for property. In these circumstances, it was a natural response.

White America was always there to say to Black America, "for you, there is no space — no space in the front of the bus, no space in this bathroom, no space in this restaurant, no space at this school, no space...no space." These 'no space' comments were common until Dr. Martin Luther King and the freedom marchers tramped their feet of freedom in those spaces.

Blacks should develop a space appreciation and property improvement plan. Blacks must take pride in their space, no matter how humble it might be; be it their house, their apartment, their yard, their car, their room, their desk, or whatever. They should determine that their house will reflect them. African forefathers were the world's greatest builders and artisans. Anything that a black becomes interested and skillful in, he will put an artistic flavor to it. Look at a black basketball player, a black football player, a black runner, a black singer, a black speaker, a black preacher, etc. If he is good at his skill, take note of the artistic way in which he performs. Blacks even walk, talk and touch each other with an artistic flavor. They must regain this flavor in everything they do.

# Chapter 13

# Community Involvement Plan

When is the family going to get involved with social and political issues? If blacks do not get out and determine their destiny, then White America will. America has had much experience in doing just that. The only way to counter that trend is for blacks to get out and get involved. They should get together as black folk and develop their own plans about issues that affect them and their families. The difference between the slave and the slave master was that the slavemaster made all the plans. If White America is still making all the plans, then she is still the slavemaster and the blacks are still the slaves. It is as simple as that. So black parents should get out and have a plan for their families.

Blacks must participate in the political process. A black parent must educate his family to the political process or assign someone in the family to be responsible for educating the family. Parents must get involved. White America is very content when blacks sit around and do nothing. Involvement is important. Blacks must understand that the political process is the American way of democracy. Voting can be power. It has taken blood, sweat, and tears to open the way for blacks to vote. To be able to vote and not do so is to function under a slavery mentality. Blacks must get out and vote. Each family should have some bright and energetic person who will be responsible for assuring that all eligible family members register and vote.

# Chapter 14

# Prevention of Perpetuation of Slavery (POS) Plan

A slogan that all blacks should engrave in their minds is, "We shall not tolerate the 'perpetuation of slavery.'"

For several centuries White America has tried to develop concepts of blacks as being inferior, and also to promote concepts of whites as being superior. Consequently, all Americans have been affected by these slavery concepts. When the average white person sees a black person, the white person's self-esteem and self-worth automatically go up. It does not matter whether the white person is tall, short, skinny, fat, stupid, wise or otherwise, his or her concept of superiority is reinforced. Whenever a black person sees a white person his or her concept of inferiority is reinforced. These feelings are automatic unless an aggressive effort has been made to counter these impressions. Why are these feelings automatic? They are such because of the slavery experience in America and the constant and continued perpetuation of concepts of slavery.

A black child and a white child are born in America. Through television they soon learn there are no black cowboys, Indians are nothing but savages, and John Wayne won the West. The educational system emphasizes similar concepts. Their early educational experiences tell them that if it's not white, then it's not good. Through the mass media (radio and television), the great perpetrators of the concept of slavery, they begin to see the black race in negative and inferior roles. In the general society, they see very few blacks in positions of authority. This constant barrage of negative images soon makes them begin to accept this fate as true. Whites and blacks both act and react on this fate. Consequently, white and black children's minds become affected by the slavery experience.

Black slaves were made to believe that anything different from White America was inferior. If their lips were different from the whites, then they were inferior. If their hair was different, if the color of their skin was different, then these things were inferior. This concept of inferiority, however, went further than just physical looks.

Blacks must accept the fact, although it is hard to stomach, that even today, most whites feel superior to blacks and most blacks feel inferior to white. Blacks must conscientiously break this cycle of inferiority. Many blacks do not realize that they subconsciously feel that way. Not to realize it is not to do anything about it. The fact that blacks have sat back and allowed America to keep them down so long verifies this. Blacks have allowed the 'perpetuation of slavery' (POS). Those situations in which White America, or blacks themselves, view themselves in an inferior way must be fought. This is not a fight of 'telling someone off.' but a fight of establishing self-value, self-esteem, self-worth, and self-quality. It is a fight of reestablishing pride, and re-educating White America. This means blacks should prepare themselves for the occasion, feel good about themselves, hold their heads high, and determine to end POS and establish themselves as proud children of God — bowing their heads to no man.

If a concept perpetuates slavery, blacks must oppose promoting it, although it may be historically true. For example: If a white person calls a black person a nigger and the black records it on tape, then every time the tape is played, he is again being called a nigger. If a young lady is the victim of a public rape, and if there were news cameras available to capture the act, it would be degrading if the tv news station continually showed the rape day after day after day and made light of the matter. To promote rape in this way is a disservice to decency. This example illustrates one of the ways in which the slavery concept is continually perpetuated. It may be called history or it may be called facts; nevertheless, it perpetuates a concept through repetition. To show the rape scene as a corrective means would be an honorable contribution, but to repeat the scene for sensationalism is exploitation, and it encourages perpetuation.

Although America should be ashamed of its slavery experience, through television, mainly she keeps feeding the monster. Blacks must fight it. America has seen enough of Uncle Tom programs. A continuation of this is not good for Black or White America. American children should not be constantly bombarded with such self-destroying information for Americans. This is not good for little white girls, little black girls, little black boys or little white boys. America should not only express shame but be ashamed of the slavery experience. She should not flaunt it.

Every black man, woman, and child should vow, every day, that he or she will not tolerate POS. They should remind themselves of this vow as they develop and interact with White America. Blacks must not tolerate POS inside themselves or outside in society.

Blacks must incorporate this slogan in their hearts so strongly that whenever a black sees a fellow black fall into the trap of slavery concepts, he must try to lift him up and remind him of the slogan "WE SHALL NOT TOLERATE THE PERPETUATION OF SLAVERY." This should be the task of every black individual, every black family, and every black church. The strongest social unit in the black community is the black church. The black church has taken a leadership role in social changes; therefore, it is not out of order to ask the churches to make this slogan a part of their prayer: "God, give America the strength and the conviction not to tolerate the perpetuation of slavery."

Social service agencies whose mission is to help those 'stuck at the bottom' should not tolerate POS. Their mission should help those who have been victims of slavery, be they black, white, red, or yellow. If the agencies are not willing to show that they will support such a mission, then we need to eliminate those agencies which receive monies for purposes of helping the needy in America.

When political officials advocate economic concerns in place of human rights and equality, blacks need to cry "WE SHALL NOT TOLERATE THE PERPETUATION OF SLAVERY." Then blacks should use their political unity to remove those officials from public office.

> "Injustice anywhere is a threat to justice everywhere."
> Martin Luther King Jr.

Some blacks may think that because they have money or education and a few white friends that they are not victims of POS. Sure, the 'house slaves' received better food, had more privileges, and in a few cases were privy to a little education, but they were still slaves and treated as such. Often, they were used to work out the slave master's purpose in perpetuating slavery. During slavery, the free Negroe's lot depended on social tolerance and not on the fact that he was supposed to be free. He was not protected by law, therefore, the things that affected the slaves also affected him. Blacks must not use their money, education, or status to put down other blacks. For in doing so, they are putting down themselves, and fostering POS for White America's benefit.

Several years ago the blacks cried, "WE SHALL OVER-

COME." At the time, that was appropriate. However, it was not clearly stated what we shall overcome. 'WE SHALL OVERCOME' is a passive stance. It implies tolerance and waiting until the opposition wears itself out. White America is not wearing out or slowing down. It just changes its tactics. Therefore, blacks need a new message - one that is more specific, more direct, and more aggressive. "WE SHALL NOT TOLERATE THE PERPETUA-TION OF SLAVERY" should be the outcry. Let there be no doubt about where they are going.

Black America must develop a sacredness for survival. Black Americans should support blacks in situations that reflect blackness. If one black succeeds, then it reflects on all blacks. Blacks must develop a true pride in their race. Lack of pride makes blacks vulnerable. Blacks must develop a stronger sense of unity. White America almost destroyed blacks once. Blacks must never allow that to happen again.

Black slaves did not have the power to overthrow slavery, but blacks today have the power to stop **POS**. They must prepare themselves and face situations with confidence. Look White America straight in the eye and call a spade a spade. Blacks should not back up, but should think positively and not look back. They should not wait until things are ready before they make their move. Some things will never be ready, unless they are made ready.

It would be a constant reminder, if after blessing the food, all family members would hold hands around the table and repeat as a commitment, "We shall not tolerate the perpetuation of slavery."

# Chapter 15
# A Word About America

Some are quick to point out that the things that have happened to the black family are also happening to the white family; that whites are displaying the same kinds of sexual behaviors; and that unwed mothers are increasing among the white population. The difference is that White America caused these things to happen to black families, but it is coming back on White America as a curse.

> "What Goes Around Comes Around"
> And, "You Reap What You Sow."

White America inflicted upon black slaves such inhumane treatment that many mothers aborted or lost their unborn babies. Perhaps millions of unborn black babies died. Today, at its own hands, America is aborting thousands of babies.

> "Lo, children are an heritage of the Lord: and the
> fruit of the womb is his reward."
>
> Psalm 127:3

Because of the savage slavery system instituted, the curse of God seems to be facing America. Abortion is now a curse to

America.

Many black slave mothers were not allowed to marry men of their choice. Large numbers of unwed mothers have been part of the black family experience since slavery, but, it is no longer just a black experience.

Many black slave mothers were forced to have several children by different men. White families are now sharing that situation. It is estimated that by 1990, the average American family will be a stepfamily. These statistics of family destruction for blacks and whites are now becoming close. This does not mean progress on blacks' part, but rather regression on the whites' part. Do not evaluate the value of an action or a behavior by the fact that 'everybody's doing it.' It does not make it right because whites are now doing it.

> "Envy thou not the oppressor, and choose none of
> his ways."
>
> Proverbs 3:31

White America sowed the wind of slavery and family destruction, and it is now reaping the whirlwind. Blacks should watch out for this new morality movement. Blacks need not get caught up in that storm. Enough damage has already been done to the black family. It is time for blacks to build.

Blacks were forced into these situations during slavery and it was a curse. It destroyed the family. White America aborted black slave babies and developed sexual breeders of our male and female slaves. But, blacks had no choice. Now blacks have a choice. They must make wise and healthy choices, while they still have the opportunity. It's time for blacks to build, not perpetuate the concept of slavery.

The slave experience for blacks in America seems to parallel the slave experience of the Israelites in Egypt. Israel was under Egypt's oppression for several hundred years. America oppressed blacks for several hundred years. The important thing to remember is that when God decided to deliver Israel with the final curse on Egypt, everyone had a choice. Those who painted the blood on the door posts avoided the curse. Those who did not were cursed, whether they were Jews or Egyptians.

One can easily see the plagues now falling on America. If blacks do not paint the blood of commitment on the door post of their homes, the curse may be theirs.

## This Generation

"That I may cause those that love me to inherit substance; and I will fill their treasures."
Proverb 8:21

Blacks must be martyrs for the cause against POS. Many are damaged physically, psychologically, and educationally, and socially because of POS. However, if the next generation of blacks has to suffer from POS, then it is this generation's fault. They must take responsibility to change themselves and White America starting now. It is time for Black America to get her piece of the pie, not the crumbs. Blacks must effectively train and teach their children that they must no longer allow White America to hand out to them the crumbs, but must go up boldly and get what is owed to Black America. She has paid her dues with lives, blood, sweat, and tears.

"A good man leaveth an inheritance to his children's children."
Proverb 15:22

# SECTION II
# BLACK HEALTH

# Chapter 16
# Black Health

After the African was snatched and stolen from his homeland and family, he experienced a tragic trip across the Atlantic Ocean. This water route to America was called the 'Middle Passage'. This trip would set a trend of bad experiences — experiences that would affect his health and the health of his descendants for generations to come.

The voyage took from 8 to 10 weeks. Some of the slave ships carried as many as 400 or 500 blacks. The black slaves were branded with a red hot iron in the form of a letter. Slaves were chained two by two. The right wrist and ankle of one slave was chained to the left wrist and left ankle of another slave. These slaves were packed in the bottom of the ship so tight that they could not sleep on their right side or their left side.

Because of the crowded conditions, the language barriers, and the insane ship owners, many of the slaves were forced to urinate and defecate (move their bowels) in the very limited space where they were chained. This area was poorly ventilated. There was very little fresh air and no sunshine in these horrible quarters. The smell of feces, urine, and the high levels of carbon dioxide, made breathing almost unbearable.

The conditions were so bad that nearly all suffered from either yellow fever, measles, malaria leprosy, small pox, pain in the head and back, chill, fever, or nausea. Chained and crowded together, men, women, and children suffered all kinds of infections. The death rate on these ships ranged from 12 slaves per 100, to 30 slaves per 100, but the average was about 16 slaves per 100.

During this voyage, the slave was served two scarce meals a day. These meals usually consisted of rice and yams, or corn meal and yams. Each slave was given one half pint of water a day. Receiving only a half pint of water a day, and losing body fluid through normal functions and sweating, yet somehow surviving, is a miracle that baffles the medical world even today. Black America, God was with you. He must have a work planned for you.

On the plantation, the black slave developed bad health habits and life styles. This happened because the slave master forced on the black slave a rigid schedule with limited resources.

> "The plantation day usually started before dawn; the slaves were roused by a horn or a gong sounded by an overseer and headed for the fields almost immediately. On many plantations they labored over the crops until about 10 a.m., when they were customarily allowed a 15 minute break to prepare and eat a simple breakfast of hoecake — cornmeal heated on a hoe held over a fire built in the open field. Late in the afternoon there was another brief interruption for a meal in the fields. Then the work continued until it was so dark the hands could no longer see. Only later that night, when the crops had been turned in and weighed, the mules tended, the wood chopped and all the master's various whims attended to, was there time for the slaves to mend or wash their own clothes, fetch their water, grind their corn or prepare another meal. And only

after that could they lie down to sleep until the horn or gong sounded another day...

"For men and women alike, rations of clothing and food were skimpy - one blanket, one pair shoes and two changes of clothes per year; a weekly allowance of cornmeal and salt pork, plus yams and fish when they were available. If his rations ran out before the week was over, the slave would have to go hungry until it was time for the next provision to be given out."

The black slave had little time to sleep, inadequate meals, unbelievable stressful situations, and a host of other experiences that contributed to bad health. They stole it, but you must return it.

Although God brought blacks through, those terrible experiences suffered by the black slave have left some lasting consequences on the health and health habits of blacks in America. The health habits and life styles that were forced on slaves became traditional. The consequences of these traditions are still affecting the health status of blacks today. In the Health United States 1985, the U.S. Department of Health and Human Services reports on the health status of blacks in America:

1. Black infant mortality (deaths) is almost twice as high as white infant mortality.
2. Heart disease is the leading cause of death in the United States. Heart disease is 20% higher in black males than in white males. In black females, heart disease is 51% higher than in white females.
3. Stroke is the third leading cause of death in the United States. The percentage of blacks in the United States that die of strokes is almost twice that of whites.
4. Over 100,000 Americans died yearly from lung cancer. The death rate for black males is 44% higher than that of white males.
5. Colo-rectal and stomach cancers were over 4

times the ratio for black females than for white females in the United States.

6. Being overweight is a risk factor for high blood pressure, diabetes, and heart diseases. In women over 35, the percentage of overweight women is twice as great for black women as for white women.

7. Hypertension is a major cause of stroke and heart diseases. In the United States, black males and females have a much higher percentage of hypertension than white males and females.

However, there are some things that you can do to lower the above figures. For example, If you have hypertension, you can lessen your chance of getting a stroke by the following:

1. Keep track of your blood pressure.
2. Do not smoke cigarettes. Smoking cigarettes will increase your chances of stroke and heart attack.
3. Do things that will help lower your blood pressure.
4. Eat an adequate diet, but watch fatty foods.
5. Exercise regularly.
6. Lose excess weight and keep it down.
7. Learn to manage your stress.

Blacks in America must look closely at their life styles and their health habits. Blacks should keep those behaviors and habits that are healthy. But, they must eliminate those behaviors and habits that spell bad health status. Blacks must cut loose the bad health habits that the slavemaster forced on the black slave.

Today some of these killers are called cultural. Once a habit or behavior become cultural, the group usually defends the habit. However, blacks must not defend bad health.

# Good Health Plan

"Beloved, I wish above all things that thou mayest
prosper and be in health..."

I John 2

## Understanding Health

The concept of good health is simple. Our bodies have millions and millions of cells. Specific cells cling together to make body tissues. Specific tissues make body organs. Specific body organs, properly put together, make the human body. So if you wish to have a healthy body, you must have healthy organs. To have healthy organs, you must have healthy tissues. To have healthy tissues, you must have healthy cells.

For cells to be healthy, they must be properly nourished and serviced. Nutrients from the food we eat, and oxygen from the air we breathe, nourish the cell. When the cell performs a function, it creates by-products or waste materials and gas. These waste materials and gas are scheduled to be discarded eventually outside of the body.

As long as the systems which service the cells are working properly and are able to bring proper nourishments to the cell, and as long as the systems which service the cells are working properly and are able to discharge the waste materials and gases from the cell, then you have a relatively healthy cell. Healthy cells make healthy tissues, and healthy tissues make healthy organs, and healthy organs make a healthy body.

Some of the main things that aid the proper nourishing and servicing of the cell are water, adequate amounts of sleep, fresh air, proper diet, meditation and relaxation, sunshine, and proper exercises. Some of the main products which interfere with having healthy cells are smoking, improper diet, excessive alcohol, and drugs.

# Chapter 17
# Proper Diet

Slave masters would give to the slave the fatty parts of the meat. Other undesirable part of the animals such as intestine were also given to the slave. The most famous was chitterlings. Chitterlings is the garbage part of the hog. But, the slave mother would take the (chittlins) and make a special meal for her family. The slave mother would use her creative talents, take the fatty parts of the meat and blend it with vegetables and make the meal very tasty. With the fat, she would make greens taste like a gourmet's delight. She would take the corn meal and make a variety of things -corn bread, cracklin corn, corn mush, corn soup, and corn pones, etc. She would take potatoes and yams, fry them, bake them, and make pies out of them. The slave mother's ingenuity, the pickled pork, salt bacon, black molasses, cabbage, peas and onions-all got the slave over.

Although very few slaves were allowed to eat a variety of fruits, some of the food that slaves were allowed to eat was as nutritious as any food. On the other hand, some of the garbage the slave owners pushed on the slaves were not nutritious. Therefore, blacks must give up these non-nutritious diets if they are to achieve better health.

Many of the foods that blacks eat today are harmful to their health. For example, the heavy use of fats and greases, used by the slave mothers to give taste and body to the meals, is a habit that is killing black folks today. During the slave experience, the slave had no choice. Today you do. Blacks must learn to prepare vegetables with much less oil and fat. From an ounce of fat, you receive more than twice as many calories as you do from other food. A high concentration of fatty substances in the blood stream is associated with hypertension and heart diseases.

Reporting on fat consumption, The Interim Dietary Guidelines by the Committee of Diet, Nutrition, and Cancer of the National Research Council states:

"There is sufficient evidence that high fat consumption is linked to increased incidence of certain common cancers (notably breast and colon cancer) and that low fat intake is associated with a lower incidence of these cancers. The committee recommends that the consumption of both saturated and unsaturated fats be reduced in the average U.S. diet. An appropriate and practical target is to reduce the intake of fat from its present level (approximately 40% to 30%) of total calories in the diet. The scientific data do not provide a strong basis for establishing fat intake at precisely 30% of total calories. Indeed, the data could be used to justify an even greater reduction. However, in the judgment of the committee, the suggested reduction (one-quarter of fat intake) is a moderate and practical target, and is likely to be beneficial." Foods of high fat content include fatty cuts of meats, whole milk, and cooking oils and fats.

## Why Is a Proper Diet Needed?

Each cell needs specific nutrients from food to perform its function. If the cell does not receive them, then it cannot do its work. If you get too many cells not doing their job, then you have a health problem. All cells do not use the same nutrients. Therefore, a well-balanced diet with the needed nutrients for all of the cells are important.

Feeding your children an unbalanced diet could result in faulty learning and below-normal intelligence. A government task force studying nutrition research concluded in their report the following:

1. Improved diets would lead to a 25% reduction in heart and blood vessel diseases. More than a million die yearly of these diseases.
2. If Black Americans would improve their diet, they could add 6 years to their life. This would equal the life expectancy of whites.

Developing a balanced and nutritious diet for you and your family takes planning, but it is not difficult. Your cells, tissues, and organs need protein, fats, carbohydrates, vitamins, and minerals in specific amounts.

## What Is a Proper Diet?

You can receive the proper amount of these nutrients by following the 'basic four food group' plan. These are four categories of foods. They are the Milk Group, the Protein Group, the Fruits and Vegetables Group, and the Bread and Cereal Group. A specific amount should be taken daily from each group.

**Milk Group**
The milk group consists of milk and milk products. This includes cheese, cottage cheese, yogurt, ice cream, and soy milk. A child should have 3 servings a day from this group. A teen-ager should have 4 cups, adults 2 cups, pregnant women 3 cups, and nursing mothers 4 cups a day. A serving is about a cup.

**Protein Group**
This group includes meat, fish, poultry, eggs, cheese, dry beans, peas, lentils, soy beans, nuts, and meat substitutes. You and each member of

your family should have 2 servings from this group daily.

**Fruits and Vegetables Group**
This group consists of dark leafy and deep yellow and other vegetables, and fruits. You and each member of your family should have at least 4 servings from this group daily.

**Breads and Cereal Group**
This group includes breads, cereals, cornmeal, grits, crackers, spaghetti, macaroni, noodles, rice and similar substances. You and each member of your family should have 4 servings from this group daily.

Eating the proper foods and the proper amounts are important to maintain good health.

# Chapter 18

# Water

On the slave ship, traveling across the Atlantic Ocean, the black slave received very little water. Once in America, the black slave was still deprived of free access to water. Often, the slave was required to travel on long trips from one plantation to another or to the auction block without stopping for water. The needs of the slave were a low priority. As long as a slave could walk, few cared about his feelings or physiological needs.

Although he worked in the fields under the hot sun, the black slave was usually allowed only two breaks a day for water and food. Eating and drinking during the same time would not allow him enough room to receive all the water he needed for all his body functions.

Many blacks today do not drink enough water. Many health problems can develop if the body does not have enough water. The slave had no choice. Today, you do.

# Why Is Water Important?

Water is essential to life. All bodily functions must take place in an environment of water. Nothing happens in your system without the aid of water. The brain operates on a mixture of air, blood sugar, and water. You could not open and close your eyes without the aid of water which moistens your eye lids. They would either stay open or they would stay closed. Water aids in respiration, glandular secretions, temperature regulation, blood circulation, bowel movements, and digestion. It takes about two gallons of liquid to digest your food daily. It also lubricates, and gives flexibility to muscles, tendons, cartilages and bones. Even your skin needs water. Death can occur when about 20% of the body's supply of water is lost.

# How Much Water Does The Body Need Daily?

A great portion of your body consists of water. This water amount could range from 50-70% of your body weight. For example, if you weigh 150 pounds, then 105 pounds of that weight could be water. This water is recycled in your body daily. If it were not recycled, you would have to drink about 40,000 glasses a day to match all the functions that take place in your body with the help of water. Water is essential. Yet, only about one percent of the liquids we drink is plain water. Lack of plain water could be a cause of obesity, diabetes, hypertension, and atherosclerosis.[35]

We lose water daily through natural functions. One hundred and eighty quarts of liquid are passed through the kidneys daily and about six cups are secreted to the bladder as urine. The skin needs lubrication and therefore, loses about two cups of liquid a day. Daily, just by breathing, we lose about a cup of liquid from the lung and through the nose and mouth. Normal bowel movement loses about a cup of liquid daily. The water losses measure to about ten cups.

These water losses have to be made up. Eating balanced meals will yield about four cups of water from the food. Oxidation of food will give the body another cup. But, to give back to the body all the water it has lost, you must drink at least five cups of liquid daily. However, no liquid replaces this body loss like plain water.

You cannot depend on thirst to always let you know that your body needs water. Therefore, you have to establish some water drinking habits. Drink at least six glasses of plain water daily and teach your children to do so. Following are some suggestions for establishing good water drinking habits:

1. Upon waking up in the mornings, drink 1 to 2 glasses of warm water. Warm water will not create a shock to the stomach. This may sound yucky (awful), but after a while it will grow on you. Persons who drink 1 or 2 glasses of warm water every morning have fewer colds.

2. Thirty minutes before each meal or an hour or two after each meal is a good time to take a glass of water. However, drinking water during a meal seems to slow down digestion. Prolonged digestion may cause some problems.

Water is also an effective agent to use outside the body. In addition to cleansing the body, hot and cold water have been used effectively in medical treatments of diseases.

# Water Substitutes

The black slave was allowed to have water although in limited amounts. Water is a basic necessity of life. But, when the black slave had the opportunity to mix water with something else, the something else with water became more attractive than just plain water. Mixing water with herbs and roots became a delicacy. Generations later, mixing water with sugar almost replaced plain water. In later generations, kool aid and soft drinks (soda pop) took over as the main beverage drink for black children. Researchers have estimated that only about 1% of all the liquids consumed today is plain water.

The problem with the kool aid and soft drinks is that they are loaded with sugar, and too much sugar interferes with good health. Sugar can interfere with the body's ability to fight off infection. The high intake of sugar affects the ability of the white blood cells to destroy bacteria. When you have not eaten any sugar, a single white blood cell can destroy 14 bacteria. If you eat 6 teaspoons of sugar at one time, the white blood cell can only destroy 10 bacteria. If you eat 24 teaspoons of sugar at one time, then the white blood cell can only destroy 1 baterium.

Speaking of sugar, the average American eats more than 35 teaspoons of sugar each day. About 30 teaspoons of that figure is more than what we need. You might say "I don't eat that much sugar." A slice of apple pie (1/6 pie) would give you 12 teaspoons. One glazed doughnut is 8 teaspoons. One can of soft drink could be around 8 teaspoons. An 8 ounce glass of lemonade has 7 teaspoons of sugar. Some salad dressings are 30% sugar. Jello is 82% sugar. Ketchup is 28% sugar. Some cereals are over 50% sugar. To preserve the food, most canned foods are loaded with either sugar or salt.

Another substance that is mixed with water that poses a health problem is caffeine. Caffeine is found in coffee and many soft drinks. It is a stimulant. Caffeine stimulates the heart, the nervous and the respiration systems. It may increase your blood pressure. Caffeine is a relaxant. It relaxes the muscles in the gut area, and the small muscles surrounding the blood vessels. It also causes the body to give up water, which leads to constipation.

Many of the soft drinks, such as Pepsi Cola, Coca Cola, and

the other colas contain caffeine. It is not advisable to allow your children to drink these drinks. Allowing this may create health problems for them in later years. In some of the cola drinks, there is about half as much caffeine as there is in coffee. Since the child's body is smaller, he is probably receiving a higher percentage of caffeine from his cola drink than you, as an adult, receive from a cup of coffee. The soda drink that contains caffeine and a lot of sugar gives your child a double dose of future health problems.

In 1983, researchers at the University of Ohio reported evidence showing that 2 cups of coffee contain enough caffeine to cause a change in the heart's rhythm and that the change could be dangerous. In 1985, the Stanford University Medical School completed a study showing that persons drinking more than two cups of coffee a day are more likely to have high blood levels of cholesterol and, therefore, an increased risk of heart disease. Researchers have also found evidence that caffeine can cause birth defects.

Do not substitute coffee for plain water. If you must continue to drink coffee in addition to plain water, use the instant caffeine-free coffees. There are also coffee substitutes that contain no caffeine.

# Chapter 19

# Sleep

For the 10-week sea passage, chained and lying on their backs, the slaves spent many sleepless nights. Even on the plantation, many of the slaves averaged only about 4 hours a night. As one slave master boasted, "I work my niggers in a hurring time till 11 or 12 o'clock at night, and have them up by four in the morning."[36] The slavemaster would often awaken the slaves unnecessarily as a preventive method of discipline. The slave had no choice in his sleeping patterns. However, you do. Many blacks today do not appreciate the importance of sleep.

## Why Are Adequate Amounts of Sleep Important?

Adequate amounts of sleep are necessary for good health. Sleep is important for the body to effectively fight diseases. Substances that fight infections, such as lymph nodes and bone marrow, are mostly produced while you are sleeping.

Proper amounts of sleep are needed to maintain mental and

emotional health. Lack of sleep causes irritability. People are more easily provoked when they lack sleep. Nerves are on edge. College students have been kept awake for days in experimental studies to see the effects of no sleep. After 24 hours, some of the students became extremely irritable. A few days later, they begin to experience memory loss. Some of the students started hallucinating after five days of no sleep. Lack of sleep can play tricks with your mind.

Sleep is important in restoring the body's energy. The skin cells divide faster and most body growth take place during sleep. Therefore, it is important that your children get adequate amounts of sleep. Many of our teenagers are allowed to stay up late at night. This is a mistake. Much growth takes place during this period and therefore, there is a need for plenty of sleep.

# How Much Is an Adequate Amount of Sleep?

We must not do physical and mental damage to our health by sacrificing our sleep. We should not allow our children to cut short their hours of sleep too soon. Children from one to two years old should get 14 to 15 hours of sleep daily. The three to four year old children should receive 12 to 13 hours of sleep nightly. The four to six year old children should receive 11 to 12 hours of sleep nightly. The six to 12 year old children should receive 10 to 11 hours of sleep.

To meet these requirements, many are going have to change their life styles. Allowing small children to stay up late, and robbing them of their sleep, is also robbing them of their physical, mental, and emotional health.

Adults who sleep an average of 7 to 8 hours enjoy the best health. Those who average six hours or less have the poorest health.[37] Research also indicates that adults who average 7 to 8 hours have a lower death rate. Adults in this group do not die as soon as those who sleep more than 10 hours and those that sleep less than 5 hours. Those that sleep less than 5 hours have the highest death rate.[38]

One out of two persons will have some type of sleep disorder. Blacks have a higher percentage of these disorders than other groups.[39] If you have trouble sleeping, try the following suggestions:

1. Exercise daily
2. Take a hot shower before bedtime
3. Let your last meal of the day be at least 4 hours before bedtime
4. Relax your body while listening to soft music or relax your mind by light reading.
5. Try to go to bed the same time each night.
6. Avoid coffee, soft drinks, and tea – those that contain caffeine.
7. Do not take sleeping pills and other drugs except as prescribed by your physician. These drugs may put you to sleep immediately, but you will usually feel worn out the next morning.
8. Do deep breathing exercises in the open air

# Chapter 20

# Fresh Air

In the bottom of the slave ship, the oxygen was replaced by odors and carbon dioxide. Inadequate heat in the slave shacks on the plantation forced the slaves to live in poorly ventilated shacks. Outside fresh air did not mean relaxation and refreshment. It meant slave work. Therefore, a congested, crowded, and poorly ventilated shack became a welcoming friend. Some blacks still resort to this type of atmosphere.

## Why Is Fresh Air Important?

From the beginning of life until death, every cell, every tissue and every organ must have oxygen to function properly. If you do not believe oxygen is important to your health, then try holding your breath for about 5 minutes. If adequate amounts of oxygen are not supplied to the brain, brain damage can result. Sometimes the damage cannot be reversed. The total nervous system is affected by a lack of oxygen. When your body cells do not receive the oxygen they need, then they cannot perform their functions properly. Therefore, when poison gases like cigarette and marijuana smoke are introduced to these cells, they either interrupt normal functions or they destroy cells.

We should practice breathing deeply outside in the open air daily. The deeper we breathe of fresh air, the more we supply oxygen to the cells. The more the cells are adequately supplied, the better the cells perform. Remember, the better the cells perform, the better will be your health. Depriving yourself of oxygen is one of the main reasons you should not smoke tobacco or be confined to an area where others are smoking.

# Chapter 21
# Exercise

Adequate amounts of exercise are not a big problem among young blacks. They run a lot. They play ball games. They ride bicycles, etc.. But, once they become adults, exercise becomes an occasional thing. Most adults who walk regularly or adults who are involved with a regular exercise program are non-blacks. The adults who play a rigorous ball game only on the weekends are probably doing more damage than good to their health. Intense physical activity once a week without other exercises at least 3 or 4 times a week puts physical stress on the body. For exercise to be beneficial, it has to be at least 4 times a week.

## Why Is Exercise Important?

Exercise is an essential body need. It may be the single most important thing you can do to live longer. The whole body system benefits by exercise. Inactive persons have twice as many incidences of heart disease as active persons. Proper exercise reduces the high risk factors for heart diseases. These risk factors include stress, high blood pressure, and elevated fats.

Diabetes is more common among inactive persons. Exercise decreases the diabetic's insulin requirements. Exercise also helps the digestive system by quicker absorption. It aids the regularity of the bowels.

Weak and brittle bones are common among persons who do not exercise. In the United States, there are over twenty-eight million persons who suffer from back pain. Eighty percent can be reversed with physical exercise.[40]

Exercise can reduce emotional tension. It promotes better relaxation, rest, and sleep habits. It gives the body greater ability to cope with illnesses.

Proper exercise gives you a stronger heart muscle. Daily exercise keeps the blood vessels open in the heart muscle that would otherwise close with age. You will have fewer fatty substances in the blood. These fatty substances can lead to hardening of the arteries, which can lead to strokes. Regular exercise can slow down your heart beat. This means that the heart does not have to work as hard. Proper exercise increases the size and the pliability of the blood vessels. It increases blood flow.

Perhaps the most important benefit of proper exercise is the improved ability of the heart, the lungs, and the circulatory system to transport oxygen to the cells. Exercise increases the body's breathing capacity. It forces greater oxygen intake, and therefore, the cells are serviced better. Food cannot be used in the body's cells without oxygen. The better the food is delivered, the better the body works. With more oxygen reaching the cell, the cell is more able to remove its waste materials, thereby, reducing fatigue and building muscle endurance.

Exercise gives the body more energy. It increases resistance to fatigue and helps counter anxiety and depression. You can avoid many kinds of pain, aches, and sicknesses if you get enough exercise.

# What Is Proper Exercise?

Walking is the best exercise to maintain good health. Walking regularly can improve your body's ability to take in more oxygen during exertion. It can increase the efficiency of the lungs and heart. Walking can also lower the resting heart rate and lower the blood pressure. Women who walk during pregnancy have shorter labors and need less medication.

You can greatly improve your physical condition if you walk about twenty to thirty minutes a day, starting at a comfortable pace.

Walking has some other practical advantages. Almost everyone can do it. You can do it almost anywhere, and almost any time.

If you are the more energetic type and choose to do more than walking, always remember that any rigorous exercise introduced to the body can be stressful. Learn to work toward your exercise goal gradually. Do not over-tax the system at the start.

If you have serious health problems, you should consult your physician before beginning a strenuous physical exercise program.

There arc several keys to a successful exercise program. Choose an activity that you enjoy so that you will continue to do it regularly. Be practical. Choose a sport you can afford and that you have the time for. Start slowly, and gradually increase the intensity and duration of the activity.

Always take time to warm up before strenuous exercising. Walking or jogging in place are good warm-up activities. Stretching can accomplish much the same goal. Stretch the muscles slowly, especially those muscles most used in the exercise. Both stretching and warm-ups get the blood flowing to the muscles which gets the system ready for the effort needed to perform the exercise itself.

Aerobic exercising has become very popular over the last several years. The object of aerobics is to use multiple muscles over a long period of time. Aerobics are not designed to increase muscle strength, but to develop the respiratory and circulatory systems.

Sports such as basketball, raquetball, and tennis are not aerobic exercises. You should be in shape before you play these sports. They call for quick bursts of energy for short periods of time and place great stress on the body.

# Chapter 22
# Stress Reduction

No one in his right mind would argue against the fact that the slavery experience for blacks in America reached the peak of human stress. The conditions under which the blacks slaves were brought to America were stress-ridden. Added to this was the inhumane way in which White America treated the slaves. The stress for blacks in America did not end with the Civil War and the Emancipation Proclamation.

Stress has been perpetuated for blacks by America. America — a country that was built on freedom and democracy. America — a country that proclaimed God as her leader. America — a country with the Statue of Liberty, with her flaming torch, welcoming foreigners to the land of the free. This is the same America that has sent out mixed and inconsistent messages of freedom to the blacks from Africa and their descendants for three hundred years. Mixed and inconsistent messages can be a major source of stress.

Mixed and inconsistent messages can even drive rats into a stressful frenzy. A classic experiment was introduced to students of psychology several decades ago. A number of rats were separated into two groups. The first group was required to pass over a specific area before they were able to receive their food. Each time they passed over this area, they received an electrical shock. Eventually, the rats adjusted to the shock. This experience did not seem to affect the rats emotionally.

The second group of rats was also required to pass over a specific area before they were able to receive their food. Sometimes, when the rats would pass over this area, they would receive an electrical shock. At other times, they would not. After a period of time, this inconsistent pattern of receiving electrical shocks and not receiving shocks made nervous wrecks of these rats. So, one can imagine the emotional effect the American experience has had on blacks.

## What Is The Stress Response?

Imagine that you are sleeping in bed and suddenly you hear someone breaking into your house through the front door. You suspect that it is a burglar. Now certain things will happen to your system. Your eyes will dilate, which will allow your eyes to let in more light. Your muscles begin to tighten up. You will start to breathe in rapid, short, and shallow breaths. Your pulse beat will increase. Your blood system will begin to carry food to your cells and the cells in turn, will cast off waste material more rapidly. Your liver will release sugar into the blood stream. Adrenaline and other hormones are released into your blood system. The blood begins to flow in greater amounts to the brain and the major muscles. The blood begins to flow slower to the stomach and to the hands and feet. Your hands and feet begin to feel cool. Your blood pressure rises. You begin to perspire. You are now ready to deal with the burglar. You are ready to either fight the burglar or to run at your fastest pace.

These body changes are nature's way of preparing you for a life-threatening situation. The burglar presented a life-threatening situation. However, if you experience these body changes too often, then these stress responses could affect you body, your nervous system, and eventually, your general health.

Not all stressful situations are life-threatening. Therefore, you must train you body not to have a life-threatening response when a situation is not life-threatening. For example, your mechanic states that the repairs on your car will cost $150, and you had expected the repairs to cost less than $75. You are on a budget, and coming up with the extra money poses a problem. This is not a life-threatening situation, and a rising blood pressure, a rapid heart beat, etc., is not going to come up with the extra money for the car repairs. You must learn to deal with non life-threatening situations without your blood pressure rising and the adrenaline flowing. It may add years to your life.

# How Can I Control Stress Responses?

One of the ways in which to control the stress response is to **Avoid** the situation. You may be able to avoid the situation that causes the stress. For example, A television program disturbs you because of its negative racial overtones. You can avoid the stress response by simply turning to another station. In some situations, it is unnecessary to get involved, so why hassle yourself.

However, you cannot avoid every situation. Another way in which to control the stress response is to **Alter** the stress in the situation. You can eliminate the stress by altering or changing the thing that is causing the stress. For example, you become very nervous (stress) when you are late and have to give a presentation. You could avoid the stress response by better planning your time so that you will arrive early and be relaxed before your presentation.

Some situations you cannot avoid or alter. These stressful situation are those you must **Accept.** There are ways in which you can accept stressful situations and minimize the stress response. One way, is to change your concept about the situation. If you know there is absolutely nothing you can do about a situation, then why worry about it.

> "Give me the strength to accept the things I cannot change, and the wisdom to know the difference."

There is nothing that you can do about the mistakes you made yesterday except to learn from them. Do not sit around and worry about them.

Another way in which to accept the stressful situation and minimize the stress response is to build your physical, mental, social, and spiritual resistance. You can build your physical resistance through proper diet, regular exercise, adequate sleep, sunshine and relaxation exercises.

You can build your mental resistance by planning your activities and life, developing some specific goals, and improving self-development and self-growth.

You can build your social resistance by strengthening the relationship with your family, establishing friends, and investing in intimate relationships.

An important way to accept the stressful situation and minimize the stress response is to build your spiritual resistance. Although things have been and still are very stressful for blacks in America, many have found a haven in the Black Church. Their belief in God and a hope of a better place, 'whose builder and maker is God,' have been a great comfort in stressful situations. Those that seem to have a deep faith in God, fare better in dealing with situations that could create stress.

Also, religious music can have soothing effects. It was the development and singing of Negro Spirituals that got many of the slaves over. Through the spiritual, the slaves experienced mental and spiritual freedom. Having a song in your heart or on your lips can help you deal with stressful situations.

# Chapter 23

# Killers

"Know ye not that ye are the temple of God, and that the Spirit of God dwelleth in you? If any man defile the temple of God, him shall God destroy; For the temple of God is holy, which temple ye are."

I Corinthians 3:16, 17

## Smoking

Cigarette smoke is a major cause of many health problems. This poisonous smoke causes 350,000 premature deaths every year which averages out to about 1,000 deaths each day. In the United States, cigarette smoke is responsible for 170,000 deaths from heart disease. Eighty percent of all lung cancer has been linked to cigarette smoking. Cigarette smoking costs more than $25 billion a year in health care. Cigarette smoke contains 160 times more cyanide (very poisonous substance) and 840 times more carbon monoxide (a poisonous gas) than is allowable in industry. Carbon monoxide is the same gas that comes out of the exhaust of a car. It can destroy body cells.

## What Happens When You Smoke Cigarettes?

1. Cigarette smoke reduces the oxygen carrying capacity of the blood. Without oxygen, cells will die.

2. Tobacco tar is composed of many tiny particles. Ninety percent of these particles contain carcinogen (cancer producing) hydrocarbons. If you smoke only one pack of cigarettes a day, you will deposit an eight-ounce cupful of nasty, sticky tar in your body each year. When this tar touches your tissues, it produces abnormal cells. Although these abnormal cells are not cancerous, these are the cells from which cancers start.

3. Nicotine causes the blood pressure to rise 10 to 20 points, and heart rate to rise from 15 to 25 beats a minute. This causes the heart to work harder. The risk of death from coronary artery disease is close to 70 percent greater for smokers than for non-smokers.

4. Cigarette smoking increases the risk of lung cancer, pulmonary emphysema, and chronic bronchitis.

5. If you smoke a pack of cigarettes a day, you will receive enough radioactive chemicals in your body to equal several x-rays a year.

## Children and Cigarette Smoke

If a couple is contemplating on having children, then the mother should stop smoking at least three months before conception. Pregnant women who smoke are endangering their unborn children's lives. The smoke from the cigarette, which contains tar, nicotine, carbon monoxide, and other poisons, enters through the mouth. From the mouth, these poisons go through the windpipe into the lungs. From the lungs, these poisons are carried into the blood stream. From the blood stream, through the placenta, the child is fed these poisons.

Parents or baby-sitters who smoke around children who are under the age of one year are affecting these children's health. Researchers have found in the urine of children who are exposed to cigarette smoke, enough concentration of nicotine to match an adult who smoked three cigarettes in three hours.[41]

Smokers should not subject little children to cigarette smoke, especially in confined areas such as cars. In cars, the concentration of cigarette smoke is high and more harmful to little children.

## What Will I Gain If I Stop Smoking?

1. Your life expectancy will increase. Persons who smoke die earlier than those who do not smoke.

2. The risk for lung cancer and coronary heart diseases decreases gradually after 10 to 15 years of not smoking. The ex-smoker's risk approaches that of those who never smoked.

## Why Is It Difficult to Stop Smoking?

Many people are both physiologically (physically) and psychologically (mentally and emotionally) addicted to smoking. When you inhale cigarette smoke, you receive a jolt to the brain in 7 seconds. Smoking a pack a day adds up to 70,000 jolts a year. That is a lot of jolts and those jolts will eventually affect the brain and the body organs.

In addition, smokers associate cigarette smoking with many things. They associate smoking with eating, drinking, stimulation, relaxation, and many other activities. Because of the long and strong associations with these activities, the urge to smoke comes automatically whenever you participate in these activities.

## How Can I Stop Smoking?

There is no one approach that works for everyone. Some can quit cold turkey, some in stop-smoking groups, and some only after they have tried several approaches. Some agencies that could be helpful are your local American Heart Association, American Lung Association, and The Seventh-Day Adventist Church.

People smoke for different reasons, have different degrees of addiction to cigarette smoking, and have different levels of motivation to stop smoking. Therefore, what works for one does not necessarily work for another. However, there seems to be some common ground for many who have successfully quit. They are:

1. They really wanted to.

2. They changed their outlook toward smoking. They did not look at stop-smoking as depriving themselves of something, but a step towards better health. Tar, carbon monoxide, and nicotine in cigarettes destroy and paralyze cells and life itself. It is as simple as that.

3. They were not discouraged by set backs, It may take time, but they were determined to eventually stop smoking.

4. They picked up healthful substitutes such as exercise, deep breathing techniques, relaxation techniques, etc.

# Alcohol

> "Wine is a mocker, strong drink is raging: and
> whosoever is deceived thereby is not wise."
>
> Proverbs 20:1

If there is one main experience that has picked up where White America left off in destroying the black family, it is alcohol. Alcoholism has destroyed many black families.

Alcoholism is a serious problem in the black community. Many blacks in their hopelessness have turned to alcohol, the hidden poison. Alcoholism has been responsible for the destruction of many relationships and homes. It is sad to see men and women, many with untapped talent, enslaved by alcohol, rising early in the morning looking for their master — alcohol. Alcohol is a demon, and whosoever plays with it will eventually get burned.

> "Give me a light!
> No, not a beer, dummy; give me some real light.
> Enlighten me with knowledge."

The high consumption of alcohol and cigarettes is killing blacks physically, emotionally, socially, and economically. It is sad that a large percentage of billboards in the black community advertise either alcohol or cigarettes. Many of our black athletes are role models for black youths. The alcohol industries recognize this. Therefore, the alcohol industries have paid these black role models to use their influence to seduce black youths through advertisement. And we wonder why so many of the young athletes are involved with alcohol and drugs.

Alcoholism is a serious public health problem. The average alcoholic life span is shortened by 10 to 12 years. Intoxication causes brain damage. In very heavy drinkers, this damage is irreversible. Heavy drinking can damage the liver. About 8 percent of the alcoholics develop cirrohosis of the liver.

The heart rate increases with small amounts of alcohol and decreases with large amounts of alcohol. Persons who drink three or more drinks a day are apt to have higher blood pressure than the average.[42] Alcohol decreases the sense of hearing and the sense of touch. Muscle coordination is slowed down.

Alcohol is also responsible for 50 percent of all deaths caused by automobile accidents, 25 percent of all suicides, and about 40 percent of all problems brought to family court.

If alcohol is a problem in your family, seek a local alcohol support group and get the family member involved in a program.

The crowning work of God's creation was man and woman. These magnificent specimens of God's creation were endowed with systems that would allow them to function physically, mentally, socially, and spiritually.

However, to function at a maximum, mankind must maintain good health habits. Those habits that promote and maintain good health are proper diet, proper exercise, plenty of water, plenty of fresh air, sunshine, adequate sleep, and faith in God. Habits that interfere with good health are life destroying substances like cigarette smoke, alcohol, and drugs. Your habits can determine your health. The slave experience in America has left long-lasting effects on the health of blacks. They stole it, but you must return it... Free your mind and body by making wise choices.

# A Final Word

BLACK AMERICA, the future can be a rich experience for you, but you will have to go for it. First, you must get your act together. Reestablish your family and establish good health practices. Black Americans possess an inner strength and sensitivity that is unmatched. Once this power is aggressively and productively released, Black Americans and the WHOLE WORLD will have a new experience.

# Appendix

## Black Man

Lyrics by Jacqueline Hokes-Neal

Black ain't white and white ain't black!
You don't need a degree to know that's a fact!
Tell me Black Man, why's that smile on your face?
When you sport them women of a different race?
Is it a status symbol, or prove your masculinity?
Educate! Escalate! It's not sexuality!
Brain pow'r! Green pow'r! makes the world revolve!
Wake up! Black Man! Think! Do! Be! — Resolve!

Stop beatin, rapin, and killin, me!
I'm on your side!
It's a shame......No one to blame.....
No where to run......No where to hide......
We're workin for the Man, earning money, trying to make it
Your're hangin on the corner, drinkin wine, scheming how to make it
Why is it, when you see your woman aimed for success,
You do drugs, waste money, and generate mess?

When I talk business, you have no rationalization
It's killing softly to see your emasculation
You're like a ship without a rudder.
But, I'll not come down to you in the gutter.
I've been laboring under false assumption
I finally woke up and used my gumption
Fact is — the Mind — ! not the behind —
That determines — the bottom line —
Heads you win! Tails you lose!

Stimulate! Motivate! Don't aggrevate that girl or boy.
Watch how you look, what you do, the language you employ.
Nurture your spiritual, physical and mental side!
Let Pride! Honesty and Integrity abide!
Man — Father — is the Child's glory!
That's the truth! It's the age old story!
When you plant that seed, Your woman conceives,
Don't pack 'n' leave. The baby's also Your responsibility!!

You have a rich heritage! You're the head of a nation.
Together we're somebody. Try recapitulation.
The sky's the limit! Be that shooting star.
Success is for you no matter who you are.
Respect yourself. Don't act a fool.
Have a pride. Remember the Golden Rule.
"Do unto others, etc." — the rest you know.
You're gonna reap just what you sow.
Take A Stand!! Be A Man!!
Be A Man!! Take A Stand!!
Be A Black Man!

# REFERENCES

[1] Peter Still, *The Kidnapped and the Ransomed: Being the Personal Recollection of Peter Still and His Wife 'Vina' After Forty Years of Slavery*, (Syracuse: Hamilton Press, 1856), pp. 153-154.

[2] Benjamin. A. Botkin, *Lay My Burden Down*, (Chicago: University of Chicago Press, 1945), p 65.

[3] Frederick Douglass, *Life of an American Slave*, (Cambridge: Belknap Press, 1971), p. 30.

[4] Williams J. Anderson, *Life and Narrative of William J. Anderson*, (Chicago: Daily Tribune Book and Job Printing Office, 1854), p. 19.

[5] Issac D. Williams, *Sunshine and Shadow of Slave Life*, (East Saginaw: Evening News Printing and Binding House, 1885), p. 63.

[6] Henry Box Brown, *Narrative of the Life of Henry Box Brown*, (Boston: Samuel Webb Bilston, 1852), pp. 16-17.

[7] Norman Coombs, *The Black Experience in America*, (New York: Twayne Publishers, Inc., 1972), p. 41.

[8] John Hope Franklin, *From Slavery to Freedom* (New York: Alfred A. Knopf, 1945), p. 65.

[9]Benjamin. A. Botkin, *Lay My Burden Down,* (Chicago: University of Chicago Press, 1945), p. 154.

[10]Gerda Lerner, *Black Women in White America: A Documentary History,* (New York: Vintage Books, 1973), pp. 46-47.

[11]Louisa Picquet, *Inside Views of Spitjerm Domestic Life,* (New York: By the Author, 1861), p. 50.

[12]Williams J. Anderson, *Life and Narrative of William J. Anderson,* (Chicago: Daily Tribune Book and Job Printing Office, 1854), p. 19.

[13]Gerda Lerner, *Black Women in White America: A Documentary History,* (New York: Vintage Books, 1973), p. 48.

[14]John Hope Franklin, *From Slavery to Freedom,* (New York: Vitage Book, 1969), p. 64.

[15]Robert Staples, *The Black Woman in America,* (Chicago Press: Nelson-Hall Publishers, 1979), p. 135.

[16]Mayo Anglou, *Jet Magazine,* (Chicago: Johnson Publishing Co. Inc., December 13, 1973), p. 18.

[17]Basil Davidson, *The African Slave Trade,* (Boston: Little, Brown and Company, 1961), p. 79.

[18]Solomon Northup, *Narrative of Solomon Northup: Twelve Years a Slave,* (Auburn: Derby and Miller, 1853), pp. 165-169.

[19]Abraham Chapman, *Steal Away: Stories of the Runaway Slaves,* (New York: Praeger Publishers, 1971), p. 158.

[20]Frederick Douglass, *Life of an American Slave,* (Cambridge: Belknap Press, 1971), p. 50.

[21]Stanley M. Elkins, *Slavery: A Problem in American Institutional and Intellectual Life,* (New York: Grosset and Dunlap, Inc., 1963), pp. 111-112.

[22]Jessie Bernard, *Marriage and Family Among Negroes,* (New Jersey: Prentice Hall, Inc., 1966), p. 70.

[23] Stanley M. Elkins, *Slavery: A Problem in American Institutional and Intellectual Life*, (New York: Grosset and Dunlap, Inc., 1963), pp. 104-128.

[24] Frederick Douglass, *Life of an American Slave*, (Cambridge: Belknap Press, 1971), p. 24.

[25] Frederick Douglass, *Life of an American Slave*, (Cambridge: Belknap Press, 1971), p. 28.

[26] Robert Staples, *The Black Woman in America*, (Chicago Press: Nelson-Hall Publishers, 1979), p. 131.

[27] Norman Coombs, *The Black Experience in America*, (New York: Twayne Publishers, Inc., 1972), p. 41.

[28] Gerda Lerner, *Black Women in White America: A Documentary History*, (New York: Vintage Books, 1973), pp. 54-55.

[29] Jessie Bernard, *Marriage and Family Among Negroes*, (New Jersey: Prentice Hall, Inc., 1966), p. 108.

[30] Jessie Bernard, *Marriage and Family Among Negroes*, (New Jersey: Prentice Hall, Inc., 1966), p. 109.

[31] Frederick Douglass, *Life of an American Slave*, (Cambridge: Belknap Press, 1971), p. 86.

[32] Robert Staples, *The Black Woman in America*, (Chicago Press: Nelson-Hall Publishers, 1979), p. 92.

[33] Margo B. Crawford, *Diamond in Dirt Theory of Slavery Seasoning the Female Slave, Perspectives on Afro-American Women*. Compiled by Willa Johnson, and Thomas Green, (Washington: ECCA Publications, Inc.), p. 22.

[34] John Franklin, *An Illustrated History of Black Americans*, (New York: Time-Life Books, 1973), p 24.

[35] Anlyan, W. Yes, "Virginia: You Can Drink Water," *The New England Journal of Medicine*, Vol 292: March 6, 1975, p. 540.

[36] John Franklin, *An Illustrated History of Black Americans*, (New York: Time-Life Books, 1973), p 24.

[37] Belloc, N. and Breslow, L., "Relationship of Physical Health Status and Health Practices," *Preventive Medicine* 1: 409-421, 1972.

[38] Hammond, E, "Some Preliminary Findings on Physical Complaints From a Prospective Study of 1,064,004 Men and Women." *American Journal Public Health* 54:11, 1964

[39] Barbara J. Combs, Dianne Hales, and Brian Williams, *An Invitation to Health: Your Personal Responsibility,* (Menlo Park: The Benjamin Cummings Publishing Company, Inc., 1981), p. 307.

[40] H. Kraus, "Diagnosis and Treatment of Low Back Pain," *General Practitioner,* 5:1952, pp. 88-92.

[41] 41*New England Journal of Medicine,* (1984) April 26:301 (17):1075-78.

[42] Klatsky, Al, Friedman, G. Sieglelaub, A. and Gerard, M., "Alcohol Consumption and Blood Pressure." *New England Journal Medicine,* 296: 1194, 1977.